THE BOOK OF SIX RINGS

Dedication

This book is dedicated to my wife and soul mate Jo, without her I would not be where I am today. She is my best friend, my support and my inspiration.

I also dedicate this book to my own students and friends—those who have stood with me in difficult times and those who have overcome their own difficulties. I dedicate it to all students of the martial way that they may find their true path amidst the turmoil of a tempestuous life.

A special mention first to my friend Andrew Beattie, for without his support, guidance, and butt-kickings I would lack training and knowledge; thanks also to Papasan.

To those that find happiness in others' suffering, who attack without justification and act through ego: the law is perfect in operation and karma is a high price indeed—ignorance affords you no protection and all debts have to be paid. Walk the path of forgiveness and compassion and be of service to humanity.

JOCK BROCAS

THE BOOK OF SIX RINGS

Secrets of the Spiritual Warrior

Life Lessons and
Intuitive Development
Inspired by the
Masters of Budo.

TUTTLE Publishing

Tokyo | Rutland, Vermont | Singapore

Please note that the publisher and author of this instructional book are NOT RESPONSIBLE in any manner whatsoever for any injury that may result from practicing the techniques and/or following the instructions given within. Martial arts training can be dangerous—both to you and to others—if not practiced safely. If you're in doubt as to how to proceed or whether your practice is safe, consult with a trained martial arts teacher before beginning. Since the physical activities described herein may be too strenuous in nature for some readers, it is also essential that a physician be consulted prior to training.

Published by Tuttle Publishing, an imprint of Periplus Editions (HK) Ltd.

www.tuttlepublishing.com

Library of Congress Cataloging-in-Publication Data

Brocas, Jock.
The book of six rings : secrets of the spiritual warrior / Jock Brocas.
p. cm.
Includes bibliographical references.
ISBN 978-0-8048-4155-9 (pbk.)
1. Martial arts--Psychological aspects. 2. Martial arts--Religious aspects. 3. Meditation. 4. Spiritual life. I. Title.
GV1102.7.P75B765 2011
796.801'9--dc22
2010042427

ISBN 978-0-8048-4155-9

DISTRIBUTED BY

North America, Latin America & Europe
Tuttle Publishing
364 Innovation Drive
North Clarendon, VT 05759-9436 U.S.A.
Tel: 1 (802) 773-8930; Fax: 1 (802) 773-6993
info@tuttlepublishing.com; www.tuttlepublishing.com

Japan
Tuttle Publishing
Yaekari Building, 3rd Floor
5-4-12 Osaki, Shinagawa-ku, Tokyo 141 0032
Tel: (81) 3 5437-0171; Fax: (81) 3 5437-0755
sales@tuttle.co.jp; www.tuttle.co.jp

Asia Pacific
Berkeley Books Pte. Ltd.
61 Tai Seng Avenue #02-12, Singapore 534167
Tel: (65) 6280-1330; Fax: (65) 6280-6290
inquiries@periplus.com.sg; www.periplus.com

First edition
15 14 13 12 11 6 5 4 3 2 1

Printed in Singapore

Contents

About This Book

I have written this book for one reason, and one reason only: to help those on their path within their chosen art to grow in mind, body and soul. I do not hold myself on the same level as great warriors and philosophers before me, and make no comparison to them. I have made my mistakes in life and learned from missed opportunities. My skills are adequate, and my knowledge is deep in spiritual truth: this is what I bring forth.

I am a simple man who has awakened. Though still a seeker of truth, I offer my little knowledge as a gift that may enhance your life. This work is for everyone, and is not restricted to those on a martial path—the lessons contained within are reflected in all areas of your life.

This book is written without judgment, and I ask that you learn not to judge lest you be judged. Remember: life is a journey of self-discovery, and you are the artist that paints your own canvas—do not attempt to paint someone else's. Allow the spiritual laws—which govern us no matter creed, color or belief—to work in perfect harmony with your destiny on your chosen path.

This book is your guide to understanding the intuitive senses within your development in *budo,* the other martial ways, or life in general. You will learn exactly what using your intuition means—not only through combat, but also in life. To be a true warrior and learn the ancient ways, you must have a pure heart (*kokorro*) and act first on the behalf of others, and lastly for yourself—this is selfless servitude. Failure to grasp this truth is why so many individuals fail to understand the essence of *budo,* and exist in the realm of materialism without truly understanding what the spirit yearns for.

The path of the spiritual warrior is not easy, and the rewards are small; yet the beauty can be witnessed if you see with the eyes of the spirit.

Jock Brocas
www.bookofsixrings.com

Introduction

It was a Sunday in September and I was in Japan, far from my home base in Scotland. My back was so painful from traveling that I could hardly walk, even after a couple of days of recuperation. Nevertheless, my teacher said, "get up and move—you're training." We traveled to Noda, and upon entering the *hombu* dojo I witnessed members from other countries talking amongst themselves. They were saying, "I hear there is a psychic medium here. Who is he? Where is he?"

Someone had already let news of my visit slip, although nobody knew that I was the object of their curiosity. I sat on the dojo floor with my heart racing and my mind running off with itself, a million miles per hour. Putting on my *tabi* shoes, I heard them speak again: "I don't believe in that garbage—it's all a scam. Where is he, is he here? Someone point him out." As I flinched, the person sitting next to me figured out my secret. To my relief, he was nice enough to keep it to himself for the moment.

I thought, *"Oh my God, what have I let myself in for? In less than an hour, I may have to take the* Godan *test."* Doubt filled me as I considered what a laughingstock I would become as the only professional psychic medium to attempt and *fail* the test of intuition. Self-defeating thoughts loomed, and in my mind I had already failed. I decided that I would "take a pass" on the test this time. As I stood up to tidy myself, the air around me changed and my crown (the main *chakra* just above my head—a spiritual gateway) went off in a spin: Hatsumi entered the dojo, smiling, his aura a ray of magnificence and full of vitality. His hair, though colorful, mimicked the crown chakra above his head and I immediately felt I had a grasp of his inner personality. He cordially greeted those around him, and as he entered he spotted me standing in the corner. He looked directly into my eyes and smiled, giving a gentle bow before walking off with a sense of recognition in his heart. I intuitively sensed that Hatsumi was one hundred percent psychic. I'm used to being the one in a group who is most "in tune," but on this day it was Hatsumi who was most in tune. He knew exactly who I was, either from vibration recognition or through his intuitive senses.

The training that day was intense, and Hatsumi continued to catch my eye. Then the moment arrived. "Anyone for the *Godan*?" I dared not move, but my good friend and teacher Andrew put a hand on my shoulder as if to say, "you'll learn something from watching this." Mischievously grinning, he shoved me forward, causing me to stumble and step up. I had no choice but to go forward, even though I felt I was not ready and I was *so* nervous—if only I could have waited a few more days! In my mind, I was calling Andrew all sorts of names—though all in good fun. Even though I felt I wasn't ready, he had faith that I could do it. I was the last in a number of individuals lined up to attempt the test. I watched failure after failure occur before my turn arrived.

I was literally shaking in my *tabi* when Hatsumi arbitrarily changed the person who was to administer the test:

"Duncan—cut." I felt relieved because I had a better connection with Duncan than with the particular *shihan* performing the cuts before him. I could see our incompatibility from his aura. This was in no way a personality issue—just an inability to connect on a vibrational level. This frustrating lack of connection would surely have caused me to fail. The chosen *shihan* was behind me and I prepared to tune in, all the while thanking my guide Ellie for being there, and hoping that she would let me know when to move by yelling in my ear when the time came. I felt a slight pushing and a vibration change in my aura, but it wasn't strong enough and no voices told me to move—I usually hear these voices clearly. My case of nerves made me feel jumpy, but when the cut finally came I reacted too late. Hatsumi stopped the class and began to teach about the *Saaki* test and how it should be administered. Mike, who was translating, said, "He can see. Sensei is saying to relax, he can see that *you* can see—relax and you will pass."

Sensei spoke about the test and the way it is important to learn how to send intention and not just feel it, and how the test is for both the test recipient *and* the test administrator. This was, of course, personal *kuden* (oral transmission) between Soke and the cutter—a kind of lesson going on telepathically, if you will. As instructed, the chosen *shihan* more keenly focused on his intent in his own way, existing in that space between life and death. The *shihan* made his cut and the next thing I felt was a rather unpleasant rush of energy that forced me to move my body out of the way—everyone applauded. I was dazed and wondered what the applause was for; I felt I had certainly failed again, but people were clapping! This experience was different from my usual psychic or spiritual experiences and I was left contemplating the distinctions: I'd heard none of the typical voices and experienced no clairvoyance. I'd only experienced sheer knowing (claircognizance). I was the only one to pass the test that day.

Whether you believe it or not, it is my opinion that this test is a psychic test, a test of intuition that takes you back to your roots to mindfully recognize who you are. Some pass, some fail, and only Sensei himself knows who has really understood the path and who has truly passed. Even on the day of my test that I've just described, Soke spoke about sensing in the aura and moving intuitively as he taught in the dojo. I believe that the vast majority of people who witness the *Godan* test do not recognize the psychic roots of this test, and when they practice, they are lost—and Sensei knows this. For the few that do understand, they have this inner knowing—a sense of completeness.

Psychic ability is exceptionally prevalent within *budo* (martial arts) and is a natural by-product of training for the practitioner who opens his or her heart to it. I am psychic: I understand it. *You* are also psychic and whether you are a skeptic or not, this book is intended to show you the reality of this truth: we are all psychic from birth and these gifts are indeed innate. Students of *budo* can develop this ability to progress further along their path of the martial way and learn to live a life that is full of happiness: abundant and blessed.

I have written this book from my heart and my willingness to share so that you may further understand your psychic sense and build this amazing capability into your training. No matter your experiences or missed opportunities in life, you cannot change who you are: a spirit having a human experience.

On the day of my *Godan* test, I was given a gift by Soke: a name and a statue. He named me "Shingan" ("divine sight" or "eyes of god"). This gift is simple, yet holds so much for me—it is not just a name but also an embodiment of who I am and who I believe you are as well. From the temple, Soke also gave me a wooden thunderbird upon which he inscribed the same name. I will always cherish that little thunderbird statue that bears the name *shinshin shingan.*

After I passed the *Godan* test, I met with Nagato Sensei during his class and we spoke about intuition and the world of spirit (to the dismay of others who had little or no understanding of this concept and were impatiently waiting to train). Nagato told me (through Tim Harrington, who translated) of a time when Soke was teaching about these special abilities and how Takamatsu Sensei was once asked to help with a police line-up in the village. There had been a murder and Takamatsu was known for his special abilities. He walked up and down the line and looked into each suspect. In so doing he was able to correctly identify the murderer. I know how he did this, and it is most certainly not a cheap parlor trick.

I am not going to show you how to identify murderers or solve missing persons cases—those activities are best left to the professionals. I will, however, show you how to become in tune with your psychic senses and adapt your studies to your chosen art. I will show you how to live a blessed life and how to make wiser life choices. I will help you to make sense of those little paranormal experiences that you may have witnessed, and most of all—if you are a skeptic—I hope to give you a little food for thought. Regardless of rank, it's easy to mock that which we do not understand, and some will revel in the misfortune of others, but these reactions are counterproductive to grasping the concepts that I present in the pages that follow. Rather, the time has come to open your heart (*kokorro*), for only with a true heart may you recognize the spiritual warrior within. *Budo* is not just about fighting; it is about living and seeing beyond the material world. True warriorship starts with compassion.

The First Ring

The Ninja and Psychic Ability

"Perception is strong, sight is weak."

—Miyamoto Musashi (*The Book of Five Rings*)

In mainstream society, there is a general acceptance of the belief that martial artists can develop abilities that seem to defy explanation. In spite of this, there is also an inclination to attempt to refute what can't be detected with the "five senses" or proven through traditional scientific methods.* However, there is a new school of thought that is emerging, and the barriers of disbelief are slowly beginning to break down. Humanity is gradually beginning to grasp that there is a correlation between science and spirituality. One can deduce that this same science is found within the martial way. In fact,

* Disbelief also comes from the fear of damnation from misguided beliefs or dogmas within religions. The mindfulness of religion is actually an exact replica of the void that we try to touch while studying *budo*, and therefore has a direct correlation to life. However, it must be understood that *budo* is not a religion, and neither is the *Bujinkan* (the international martial arts organization headed by Masaaki Hatsumi in Japan). *Budo* is a way of living: of becoming the warrior within and the spiritual warrior without.

the division between the science of *budo* and its associated spirituality is a veil that is extremely thin indeed, and with proper understanding and training the veil will be broken through. Whether or not you believe in the sixth sense (intuition), it *is* there, and here's the reality my friends: it will eventually force you to recognize it when you least expect! It may even save your life—unbeknownst to you or those around you. My very good friend Ed Martin, a.k.a Papasan (or Granddad as I call him), had this very type of experience, which perhaps encompasses what it is all about.

> *I am alive today because I listened to a voice that clearly spoke to me inside my head. I'll explain. About eight years ago I had begun riding my bicycle for four miles each day I was at home. One day, during the summer of 2000, I had departed for this daily ride and had gone about one half mile from my home. I was pedaling up a small hill and beginning to breathe rather heavily when a voice went off in my head. It said, "Ed, get off this bike or you will fall off." I pulled over to the side of the road and got off. The next words the voice spoke to me were, "Ed, lay down or you will fall down." I laid myself down on the grass and remember popping the strap on my helmet and that is all.*
>
> *The next thing I knew, a couple had parked their car and were walking across the grass to me and asking if I was all right. At that point my mind was crystal clear but my body was too weak to get up. I didn't even know I'd passed out until I realized that my bowels had let loose and I'd fouled myself. They called both my wife and emergency services. Both arrived very quickly and by then I could stand, so after first going home to clean myself, I went to the hospital.*

It was found that my aorta valve had closed to 6/10 of a centimeter in diameter (down from the average two centimeter opening). I was receiving only a fraction of the life-giving blood that should have been flowing to my body and brain. I had already gone into oxygen debt and if I had not listened to that "voice," I would have died right there on the street. Anyone who has had such an experience no longer questions the existence of such senses—they would be a fool to do so. For all others, it is much better to keep an attitude of "suspension of disbelief" than to refuse to accept such a possibility. I urge you to keep such an open mind.

—Ed Martin (Shihan)
Kudan Bujinkan Ninjutsu

I remember watching those ninja and martial art movies when I was a kid and I particularly remember all the supernatural abilities that a ninja or even a master of kung fu was supposed to have—abilities such as sensing danger, increasing stamina and strength, and controlling the minds of opponents during combat. Even though I have been naturally psychic since birth, I have never viewed what I can do as "supernatural" and as far as I am concerned, paranormal *is* normal. As a child I yearned to be a ninja or a kung fu master and develop these super powers—much to my mother's chagrin. Like every other kid on the block, I used to go around trying to emulate what the ninja were doing in the films. My mother even had some very expensive collectible coins that I threw away by using them as ninja *shuriken* weapons, and I destroyed many of my mother's gardening tools as I used them "in battle"—I suppose she can thank Hollywood for that.

Yes, the ninja do have special abilities, but they are no different from any other dedicated martial arts master, or anyone else, for that matter. The ninja were simply aware of nature and the totality of the universe. They developed their intuition through the study of nature and meditative practices, and they continue this study even today. I am still a kid at heart, but now I know the real path is a journey of self-discovery and not of technique: it's about seeing the beauty in the flower—and not just the flower in front of you. The perception of the *kosshi* or "essence of life" is to see beyond the physical plane of existence. To get caught up in technique keeps us prisoner to rational thought, and so we only move in a rationalistic manner. I know that with dedication and understanding, you can develop your intuitive senses through training, meditation, and what Hatsumi terms as *kokorro* ("heart") or *kyojitsu* ("truth/falsehood").

In Japanese culture, the ninja (originally known as *shinobi* or *shinobi-no-mono*) became legendary warriors known for their unconventional skills, but less known for their spirituality. Mention the word "ninja" and many individuals will tell tales according to their understanding and what they believe they know or what their perception is. One common definition of a ninja would be, "a super-samurai who was an expert in spying, assassination and the occult." This definition is not surprising, as the ninja is often depicted as a sinister, black-clad warrior who was an expert in the occult and in guerrilla warfare. This image could not be further from the truth.

Unfortunately, this misunderstanding is still prevalent for many people. I have had a few individuals come for their interview to join my dojo but who have been turned away because their understanding was clouded by fantasy and mysticism. I no longer teach regular classes, and do not have an open door policy. I only accept personal students who have a desire for real growth. I suppose it is very handy to be as psychic as I am because I can identify the hunger within the person's spirit and make a decision based on the person inside rather than the person outside. It's wrong to judge without evidence, and we must see the spirit rather than the physical being. In so doing, I offer the keys to the doors of change, and it is within the individual's free will to choose them.

That's not to say that I have not dealt with my fair share of "Walter Mittys" and dreamers. I remember walking into a new class I was starting and my head student said to me that "quite a character" had just turned up, his eyes raised a little to show me his annoyance—I knew what he meant instantly. As I approached the individual, I could see a young man dressed as a black-clad, sinister assassin (or so he thought) and I nearly wet myself trying to contain my laughter at the ridiculous vision that stood before me. I took him into the little office where I hold my interviews and asked him, out of politeness, why he wanted to train with us. He told me he wanted to learn the art of the assassin and how to disappear. Not one to disappoint, I told him to go a different class up the road.

On another occasion I was faced with a rather gaunt and Gothic looking guy who had long black fingernails, eye shadow, and black lipstick. I didn't really like his energy and this feeling was validated when I spoke with him. "What's your name?" I asked. He replied, "the Prince of Darkness," and with that, my decision was made. I told him to try another art or find his creative expression elsewhere.

We run across all types of people in life and some can be quite misguided. It is important to quickly and accurately discern between right and wrong, and good and evil. Even though someone may appear to be "trouble," a good heart may beat within. Determining which sort of individual you are dealing with provides you with an opportunity to use your natural intuitive ability. At one point an individual named Steve came to my dojo, and he projected the image of a "bad boy" whose aura told a story of hardship, despair and pain. I have a great reputation with local law enforcement and have trained many officers, so one of them approached me to tell of Steve's rap sheet that "ran the length of his arm," indicating that he would be a danger in the dojo. Steve was known to have anger issues, to boot. The officer was convinced that Steve would use the training for bad deeds. I talked with Steve for a while and psychically, I could see that the young man was suffering from severe loss. I knew this by the way the spirits of deceased family members—especially his brother, who had passed away through a drug overdose—had "popped in" during our conversation to see what was going on. I could see—psychically—that the young man had the desire to change his life and his rough persona was only a by-product of a negative environment and influences beyond his control. I decided to give the guy a chance. I would love to say that this little story has a tidy ending, but I can't. Steve trained for a while and became a respectful student, but pressure from certain elements of local law enforcement would not permit him to continue. Sometimes individuals in power do not know the difference between compassion and understanding. However, I can tell you that somewhere in Scotland there lives a certain once-troubled young man, with a new baby and a wife. Ever since our meeting he has steered clear of trouble, despite his ineligibility to train. I still hear from him now and again. Although he was once a skeptic, he was happy that his family came—in spirit—to say "hi." He characterizes our fateful first meeting in the following way: "The talk you gave me that first night changed my life. I did not know what a warrior was before we met." I could have ignored my vibes and perhaps consigned the young man to learning some difficult lessons in prison. Instead, even the short time spent training together was enough to set him on a new path—all because I ignored the popular opinion and followed my intuition instead.

One final note before we move on: the Japanese character *nin* can be translated into many meanings but is normally recognized as "the art of stealth" (also translated as "*shinobi*"). Some of the other meanings are *perseverance*, *endurance*, and *sufferance*. The ninja and many other *budo* masters endured many physical hardships. However, more important is the way that they endured *spiritually* and perhaps learned great wisdom from the natural order of the universe.

A Brief History of Ninjutsu

There is a great deal of conjecture surrounding the history of the ninja. Many scholars have tried to understand their history. Books have been written and the details in the stories vary with each new author's unique perspective. Another factor that tends to cloud the issue is the large number of clans that purported to have taught traditional ninjutsu or to have had a lineage that proves the history.

Ninjutsu's humble beginnings came from the samurai classes and developed over many years. The lineage clearly dates back more than 1,000 years, and evidence suggests that the art can be traced back beyond 4,300 years, making ninjutsu one of the oldest (if not the oldest) living martial arts. I use the word "living" here with some authority, as ninjutsu continues to evolve to this day.

There are nine schools of ninjutsu, each with its own history and lineage. The Bujinkan system comprises these nine schools and makes up the system. However, there are rumors that there are more than nine schools, and that the unaccounted-for traditions are intentionally kept secret. Perhaps this is true, and perhaps not, but it certainly gives you cause to think. I have listed the commonly accepted schools and have chosen not to delve into their individual histories as that would go beyond the scope of this work. If you wish to know about the history of the individual schools, investigate some of the excellent literature that is available.

The nine schools are as follows:*

- Togakure Ryu Ninjutsu
- Gyokko Ryu Koshijutsu
- Koto Ryu Koppojutsu
- Shinden Fudo Ryu Dakentaijutsu
- Kukishin Ryu Happo Hikenjutsu
- Takagi Yoshin Ryu Jutaijutsu
- Kumogakure Ryu Ninjutsu
- Gyokushin Ryu Ninjutsu
- Gikan Ryu Koppo Taijutsu

Psychism within the Martial Arts and *Budo*

Psychic ability within the martial arts has always existed but has been known by and labeled with different names such as: *sensing, saaki, mu,* and many others. The important thing to note is that psychic ability or natural intuition can be thought of as a by-product of the study of the ancient ways, and you must also accept that it is not the only *way*—and religion is not the only path either. The same can be said for activities or studies that lay outside the remit of the martial way. For instance, one could attain the same type of enlightenment through sheer dedication to another particular path. The correlation is this: every path eventually leads to the same end.

The importance of being able to sense danger within the martial arts is useful not only for self-preservation but in

---

* Adapted from Masaaki Hatsumi's *Ninjutsu: History and Traditions*. Unique Publications, 1982.

order to remain safe from injury and evil acts. Yet the student on the path through *budo* often disregards this important facet of training, holding instead to the mindset of learning technique after mechanical technique—only developing the physical self to the detriment of the spiritual self. Many other teachers who I have spoken to contest that physical training will help to develop sensory perception or higher levels of awareness. Unfortunately, I cannot concur. Purely physical training will only promote higher levels of awareness within the physical realm and not a spiritual one. There must be the adjoining of all facets of mind, body and soul. In this way, we can transcend material perception.

Hatsumi will often say, "Techniques don't matter, if your intuition isn't working—you will be killed." That may sound like quite an extreme statement, but it does bring to light the importance of developing intuition to improve your development in your chosen art or *budo*.

Allow me to explain—in layman's terms—how you can use intuitive guidance within your martial training. Any martial arts instructor can teach you the fundamental basics of *reacting* to an attack. However, it is far more productive to *anticipate* the attack by listening to your sense of intuition. While initiating an attack, there are two things that occur: first, the attacker will manifest the thought that consciously tells him to attack. After the thought is manifested, a nerve impulse will travel through his body, which will result in the physical movement. Consider this thesis: by using your innate intuitive senses, you can anticipate the movement by tuning into the energy of the aggressor's thought, or, as Hatsumi and other *budo* masters will say, "the intention." In this way your body will react subconsciously and will not wait for the conscious breakdown of all the outward elements of the attack in progress.

How Ninjutsu Is Misunderstood

Today ninjutsu, and even *budo*, seems to be misunderstood to varying degrees. To prove this you need only make a brief foray onto the World Wide Web to witness the confusion for yourself. You will find a lot of conflicting information and plenty of arguments along with personal attacks on students and teachers by spiritually weak and ill-informed individuals. A great many martial arts students tend to mock what they fail to understand. But I ask, why is it that many accomplished martial artists find *budo* and "get" the missing link? There must be a reason that so many do. I have studied other arts but have found that none of them traditionally encompass the aspects of mind, body and spirit as a whole in the way that *budo* does. Of course, the other arts' traditions of spirituality are always there, but one component often remains missing: a teacher who understands spirituality—not only in theory but in the daily walk of life. There are many inadequate teachers who I would like to name here, but that would be unspiritual of me and that is not my true nature, therefore I will let natural law play its inevitable role.

There is far more to gain when you embark on a journey within *budo* than in many other avenues that you might pursue, though I am, of course, allowing my bias to show in writing this. However, individual spirituality is understood through experience and not theory. You will develop spiritually without realizing it, and you will become more sensitive to energy and movement in the technique of your choice, and therefore be able to grow. The process will be similar to the way a small seedling develops into a strong tree as long as all the requisite resources are present.

I often tell students who have trained with me for a while to go and choose a bonsai tree or another plant that they are drawn to. I prefer the bonsai as it represents everything that the totality of the universe is; it is life, it is impermanence, energy and the roots needed to grow. When the right nutrients and conditions are given, it will grow into a strong tree with deep roots and vibrant life energy. Surely this is a goal of our training in *budo*. The Tree reflects the *kosshi* (essence) of *budo,* including *Sanshin no Kata* (five elemental movement forms) and *Kihon Happo* (basic eight methods of dealing with attacks). *Sanshin* represents the elements if you will, or the conditions required, and the *Kihon* can be understood as the roots of your *budo*. One needs the other to exist and to have balance. I make comparisons to these elements of our training and tell the students that the tree represents life, and just like the very basic techniques of the *Kihon Sanpo*, if we tend it lovingly and recognize its ethereal power while giving it all the necessary nutrients, it will become robust and develop strong roots to give it a good foundation. This is exactly the same as in *budo*: when we begin our development, we are mere seedlings and need to be fed with the right nutrients to become strong and fruitful in our quest. If you do not tend the tree with loving care, empathy and understanding of its nature, it will die—and this is also representative of your understanding of *budo* and the very nature of the martial ways.

In the modern world, we are faced with the bastardization of tradition, which is sacrificed for sport and entertainment. For instance, let's take MMA (Mixed Martial Arts), which is a blood sport with little moral value (this is, of course, my opinion). The spirit of *budo* is replaced with ego and negative emotion, which engulfs and destroys one's martial spirit. I have had some competitive MMA fighters come and train with me, and they've admitted that they feel like they're losing tradition to entertainment, and they realize that their actions as entertainers have little to do with authentic traditional combat arts or spiritual awareness. They are consumed by egoism and fail to recognize that the warrior spirit within them is diminished due to materially driven motivations. Ultimately, many of these fighters follow their convictions, leave MMA, and pursue traditional martial arts.

Mastering the Ego

The ego is perhaps the nemesis of the student of *budo.* Rather than fighting a losing battle against it, we should learn to understand it, love it, and control it. The ego, when left without control, creates separation from the divine energy that you are; it brings about disparity, despair, heaviness, materialism and a general sense of dissociation from humanity—ultimately, it engenders a lack of love and compassion. The ego is part of us and helps to maintain balance, rather like a yin and yang or good and evil—one part cannot function without the other. Isn't it true that a great many students of the martial ways are full of ego and cannot see beyond the art that they study, always picking fault with the techniques of others? In Buddhism there are many *dharmas* and it is said that there are 84,000 doors that open to the right path or way. Perhaps we should imagine the same analogy in our *budo* and realize that every *ryu ha* (school) has something to offer. No one school represents the only way to salvation. In essence, there are many doors to choose from and instructors, as spiritual teachers, are there to help you unlock the door of your choice.

Few actually understand the essence of what *budo* represents and many *budoka* can't understand why some *shidoshi* (teachers) and indeed *shihan* ("gentleman teachers" or masters) neglect to recognize the essence of spirituality that is encompassed within this facet of *budo* and the martial way. Spirituality must coexist with the other physical aspects of *budo* and in this way, we are truly alive—similar to the way that meditating while training is the essence of *budo*. Within any system there are some who will pass judgement on others and fail to see their own shortcomings, choosing instead to cause suffering in others. This is a problem with many non-spiritual *shihan* in particular. I have been a target of this type of behavior myself. Allowing this behavior to continue is like giving alcohol to the alcoholic—it feeds the negativity in their soul. This type of person will typically attack without provocation or justification, and will spread gossip and malicious talk outside of school. I am sure that I'm not the only one who has experienced this, but a truth of life is that karma will settle all "debts." Of course, there is also human law, which exists to protect you and again this is the yin and yang of things. It is important to recognize that your mind, body and soul can't grow if you fail to identify your own weaknesses or if you enjoy seeing others suffer. It is by confronting these weaknesses that one learns and develops. In my mind, there is no such thing as a mistake—only an opportunity for real growth. Do you often find yourself noticing weaknesses in others? Perhaps they're a reflection of your own shortcomings, and an opportunity for you to develop spiritual understanding.

The ego will keep us locked in a battle between spirituality and materialism and will be the little voice that continually echoes weaknesses or self-defeating beliefs in our ears. In order to change, we must accept who it is that we are and what our ego is trying to achieve. You must remember that energy is a constant in motion and as such, so too is the ego. The fundamental difference is that we can control the ego through force of will and recognition of our own spiritual authority. One counterproductive function of the ego is to destroy your belief in yourself and your positive emotions, therefore gaining control of your will. Allow me to give an example: Let's say you have been studying for many years to become a surgeon and you have passed all the theory exams with flying colors. The day comes when you have to carry out a surgical procedure on a live person and you choke, shake, and fail to live up to your own expectations. What has happened? Quite simply, you have failed to believe in yourself. No matter how much theory you understand, if you do not believe in yourself and your natural ability, you will fail to realize the goal you set out to achieve.

In the dojo, your ego will tell you that you are not good enough and that everyone is better than you. It will make you turn from your true path as you desire material successes and not spiritual growth; you will be locked in a battle between technique and the spirit (essence or *kosshi*). Instead of persevering and enduring, you will envy the person who is more skillful; you will fail to see the beauty in the movement or capture the essence of the technique—for within the spirit or essence is the doorway to enlightenment. You will give way to form and not intuition. Perhaps you will begin to judge others without realizing that we are all learning and judgement is the path to destruction. You will be driven by emotion rather than heart-centered belief. The ability to change and have all that you deserve will be diminished if you allow your ego to control you. By developing the psyche (soul) you become empowered to be who you are meant to be—to recognize the interconnectedness of all that pervades the universe. If you learn to control the ego and allow your psychic gifts to develop you'll make wiser life choices, move intuitively, and most importantly, you will sense problems before they occur.

Problem Egos Abound

You may have your hands full with your own ego—learning to tame that little monster can be difficult. But there will come a time when the others' egos will begin to affect you negatively, in small or profound ways. The martial arts are fraught with battling egos. The ego-controlled individual will always ridicule your abilities, holding you up as an example of poor quality. However, you will find that this only reflects their weakness back on them. Who cares if your technique or understanding leaves something to be desired? The truth is that you are on the path of discovery and you learn as everyone does.

The ego-driven person will naturally attract those who share their own vibration and poor spiritual posture. You will often find them setting themselves up as a "champion" for what they perceive to be right, when in fact they are showing themselves to be lacking in compassion and real understanding of *budo*. They act as delusional judge and jury on all matters pertaining to the art they choose. They're often found dictating other aspects of life and indeed others' lives outside of the dojo (and online, in forums).

The true warrior will show pity and compassion and realize that these egos need tending in a loving way. Endeavoring to respond this way is the epitome of spiritual warriorship. However, armed with spiritual power, you will rise above these trials to feel the true warmth of *budo*'s flame—not the cold perception of weak-minded ego, which cloaks itself in inner turmoil and ignorance of spiritual reality.

Budo Is a Pattern for Life

The study of *budo* or traditional martial art—can be thought of as a pattern for life, for within the schools and the philosophy is all that you will need to survive in life and to spiritually grow—it truly is the art of living and loving. It can take a while before the mind perceives what the eye can't physically see, and this is the challenging journey that we all embark upon. Everything that you learn within *budo*, the Bujinkan or indeed other traditional martial arts gives you the necessary tools needed for change and manifestation. Anything that you experience in life can be a reflection of your lessons within the dojo. Consider any problem that you face in life: because we deal with challenges emotionally, the problem will manifest as difficulty in your physical and spiritual training. Of course, the result of all these lessons is perseverance and endurance in all things, and so through training you will learn the real meaning behind the character *nin*.

The Lessons of Experience

I can speak from experience when I tell you that out of 100 *budoka*, probably only five individuals have actually experienced real combat, either on the battlefield or face to face with an adversary. Fighting in the ring is different than survival on the street. You know that the risks of dying in the ring are relatively negligible. In comparison, the risk of dying in a street fight is quite a bit higher. The unlucky few with life-and-death combat experience can attest to the surge of adrenalin felt in the face of a violent assault. Most who claim to have experienced this are all talk. Not to state the obvious, but it hurts to get hit! Being able to move intuitively can save you a lot of pain, and may even save your life. There are many martial artists who are what I would term "technicians," and they know techniques and theory like the back of their hands. However, they fail to connect with the essence of their art and so become locked in the rationale of the moment. Don't wait to find out the hard way: knowledge of techniques alone will not keep you alive—your intuition *will*.

The Second Ring

Meditation—A Gift of Nature

"What we think, we become." — Buddha

Nature holds many secrets, but the paradox is that there are no *real* secrets because those "secrets" are there for anyone to find—if they would only open their hearts and inner eyes. The secret and the wisdom comes from your own divinity. The sages of the ancient civilizations and the masters of the martial arts have always found this wisdom through nature herself. Many still believe that this wisdom is mystical, esoteric, and for only the very blessed, yet the truth is that the wisdom is there for everyone to find. What is this "wisdom?" Quite simply, it is a lesser form of being *enlightened* and it enables you to recognize your place within the universe. So, we become spiritual warriors of enlightenment, and not warriors who are solely reliant on physical prowess and skill. The spiritual warrior is devoid of egoism, compassionate, and understanding. The spiritual warrior also holds great wisdom, has empathy, is forgiving and, above all, compassionate. In the words of Sri Sri Shankar, "Enlightenment is the Journey from the head back to the heart, from words back to silence."

For thousands of years, warriors from every race within humanity have understood the advantages of spiritual development and intuition to further develop and strengthen their skills of warriorship—perhaps even giving them an advantage in battle.

Unfortunately, in our materialistic world, the modern warrior is apt to rely on ever-prevalent techniques, becoming nothing more than a technician rather than an intuitive warrior. Moving seamlessly from A to B to reach the destination at C seems like nothing more than acting according to a series of learned movements directed to work against a certain prescribed attack. The truth is that these scripted attacks are never real; they are merely a pale reflection of nature.

Even within a ring or on the mat at the dojo there is still an element of predictability. Conversely, as with Mother Nature and her own innate randomness, a true attack in an unfamiliar environment is as chaotic and unpredictable as waves on a beach. The problem we face is that if we do not learn to move in a natural way—heightening all of our intuitive gifts—we can become victims of our own folly and limit ourselves to predictable movements. You become nothing more than a tactician instead of a musician. In short, we bring about our own demise by failing to understand the natural force of the universal energy. What do you see if you stand at the side of a river? Do you see the river in all its physical glory, or do you see its natural flow and energy, as nature intended? What you perceive may be different from what your spirit sees—look with the eyes of a sage and the heart of a warrior to see that nature exemplifies the natural flow that should exist in our technique or philosophy within the dojo.

How do we achieve this brand of perception? It doesn't follow that we have to understand where a hand is placed or a foot is placed, but that we react according to the energy that flows toward us. Placement becomes displacement and learning to understand the flow of our energy ensures our natural flow and reaction to the energy in that place and time. When we reach this pinnacle of understanding we can also predict the nature and outcome of the event, or perhaps change the course of the event's history. The first principle to understanding energy is to join with it by learning to meditate. Energy within the martial arts—and other esoteric arts—has many names, but we shall refer to it as *ki*, which is the Japanese character for energy.

What Is This Energy—*Ki*?

We all understand energy differently, but suffice it to say that modern science has found that the energy that exists is part of us, and permeates all things. This has been recently "discovered" by science, yet many spiritual individuals and *budo* masters have recognized the truth for thousands of years.

Lynne McTaggart writes, "Human beings and all living things are a coalescence of energy in a field of energy connected to every other thing in the world. This pulsating energy field is the central engine of our being and our consciousness, the alpha and the omega of our existence. 'The field,' as Einstein once succinctly put it, 'is the only reality.' "*

This energy consists of atoms that vibrate at a tremendous rate that we cannot perceive with our physical senses. We can, of course, use our spiritual sense to feel this energy. In relation to the human body, this energy surrounds us and is known as *the field*, which consists of many layers.

The energy, *ki*, is known in China as *qi*, and in India as *prannha*. No matter what the term, this energy is part of us,

* From *The Field: The Quest for the Secret Force of the Universe* by Lynne McTaggart. HarperCollins Publishers, 2003.

surrounding every living thing. It is also important to recognize that many renowned scientists, such as Dr. Barbara Brennan (an ex-NASA physicist) have scientifically proven the energy's *aura*, and Russian scientist Semyon Davidovich Kirlian was the first to photograph it. This aura is the medium through which we are able to sense subtle changes in *auric vibration*. Being able to understand how the *ki* works is the first step toward developing your intuitive senses within *budo*.

Let's look at the makeup of the aura and how it can aid us in protecting our mind, body and spirit. From my years of training as a psychic and student of *budo*, I've learned that the energy field consists of rings of energy,* We shall deal with four of these layers, though there are many more, each with its own job:

Etheric—This is the first layer that most psychically gifted individuals can see. It extends approximately half an inch from the body and almost acts as a second skin. Within this layer, physical ailments can be detected. It looks silvery blue in color although some see the color as gray. This layer also holds the blueprint of your physical body. You can easily train yourself to perceive this energy. I always show my students how to see the aura of a line of trees in perhaps a field or a living forest. If you look at the top against the white background of a cloud or blue sky—you will notice the energy at the top of it—a kind of haziness that surrounds the living object like a halo. Next, you should try to visualize the same layer around a companion in the dojo by getting them to stand against a light background while you focus your attention around the area immediately surrounding their body.

---

* From *Power of the Sixth Sense* by Jock Brocas. O Books, 2008.

Emotional—This layer contains the emotions you are feeling at any moment, so the colors within the aura can change according to how you are feeling. So, if you are feeling depressed or low then the aura will reflect the vibration and color that matches that emotion. How can this emotional state effect the ability to look after your mind, body and spirit? If you are feeling the emotion of fear, then you will exude that emotion and any sensitive individuals will be able to pick up that emotion. This layer also exudes the emotion that we feel for others around us—so if you are feeling anger at someone, then that emotion would be easily recognizable. This can serve as an early warning sign to you if you learn how to recognize the emotional state of others.

Mental—The mental layer contains the information on your beliefs, intellect and personal power relating to the sum total of who you are in the physical and mental sense. Thought processes are registered in this area—your decisions and opinions are registered in this field. The color of this field is mainly yellow and thought forms are structured as amorphous blobs of energy. The thought forms that are in our awareness at any given time are registered in this field. Obviously, with training and raised awareness, we can pick up on these thoughts through the sixth sense.

Spiritual (*Astral* Layer)—This layer is the bridge to the spirit world and receives all information via channeling the higher vibrations through the *crown chakra* ("*chakra*" is a Sanskrit word meaning "spinning wheel"), which is situated just above the head. These *chakras* are like vortices of energy that run from the base of the spine to above the head. They are also known as the psychic centers, of which there are seven. However, it must be noted that ancient wisdom and teachings suggest there are far more. The crown *chakra* also works in collaboration with all other *chakra*s but is more emphatically connected to the *heart chakra*. It is through these layers that all thoughts and intentions are perceived. For instance, there is an anatomy of thought. This anatomy of thought explains how the physical manifestation occurs.

The interaction between both the subconscious mind and the conscious mind requires similar collaboration through the nervous pathway of the body, though one is, in essence, the same as the other, much like matching facets of a diamond. For instance, the cerebrospinal cord is the channel through which we exercise conscious nervous command such as that seen in the movement of limbs. This is control of the physical senses in order to bring about the action of a particular movement. This particular system has its nucleus in the brain, yet the brain is entirely separate from the mind. The sympathetic nervous system has its center in a network of nerve cells at the back of the stomach known as the *solar plexus*. In spiritual terms this is also known as the *solar plexus chakra*, which is the seat of intuition and psychic ability. This system channels unconscious mental activity and also supports the vital functions of the autonomic nervous system. These two systems are connected through the *vagus* nerve, which passes out of the cerebral region of the brain and through the throat where the *throat chakra* is situated. It then branches out to the heart and lungs and joins with the sympathetic nervous system making the physical body a "single entity"—the mind and body.

Each nexus of the central nervous system coordinates with one of the seven corresponding basic *chakra*s. There are also many other *chakra*s around the body that are listed in ancient Sanskrit teachings. The progression of *chakra*s begins at the head or cerebral area, identified as the crown *chakra*, which is your connection and bridge to the realm of spirit. It then continues to the *third eye chakra*, which is located at the forehead and works in conjunction with the pituitary gland, yet also remains autonomous—this is the seat of clairvoyance and the ability to perceive what is unseen. The next area is the throat *chakra*, which is the area at the throat and remains the seat of clairaudience (our ability to hear spirits). If we continue down we reach the heart *chakra* and the solar plexus *chakra*. Each of these *chakra*s works in partnership with the sympathetic nervous system. The heart *chakra* is one that is associated with unconditional love. We then continue to what could be described as the physical anchor of the spiritual body, which encompasses a further two *chakra*s—namely the *sacral plexus chakra*, based just below the naval and concerned with intuition, and finally on to the back and the *root chakra* situated just below the groin area, which is the connection to the material world. These two *chakra*s are in tune with the physical elements of the body, and so all work in concert as mind, body and spirit.

So it is true that subconscious thought can effect changes in the physical body. Perhaps then, this is the basis to effect spontaneous healings within an individual or the method by which we are able to change our outlook and circumstances in life.

Understanding the physical path of thought and perception can help us correlate the spiritual with the physical. Thereby, we are able to learn, co-create, manifest, feel intention and endure through emotional turmoil.

According to Thich Nhat Hahn, "Each thought, each action in the sunlight of awareness becomes sacred. In this light, no boundary exists between the sacred and the profane."*

---

* From *Peace is Every Step* by Thich Nhat Hanh, Bantam Books, 1991.

Nin—Perseverance and Endurance

I am leading up to one of the most important spiritual lessons of all within *budo*. This lesson is so important that it is probably the basis by which the masters of *budo* succeed, and develop their intuitive side as well as their spirituality. That lesson? *Nin*. The first characters of the *nin kanji* can be translated as "perseverance" and "endurance." At first, you could be forgiven for labeling this attribute as an aspect of your physical training only.

What does it mean to persevere and endure? Perhaps to understand *ninpo* (the higher wisdom of the ninja) we need to endure and persevere not just through our physical training but also in all of life's lessons. It is important to see and feel the *nin* in everyday life. For instance, is it ever right to give up on anything that makes you happy just because you feel the pinch for a while? This is not perseverance. In the midst of life's struggles, we sometimes give up or change what we want to suit the emotion of the moment. It is easier to give up than to persevere and endure.

This can be likened to the struggles of a newborn horse. Time and time again the young foal will try to get up on its shaky legs until it finally succeeds. Within its natural inner makeup is the sense of perseverance and endurance. Rather than just sit there in a heap of failure, the foal will eventually stand up by its own volition.

Enduring through Emotions

A great percentage of us give up when experiencing negative emotions: we succumb to negativity when confronted by seemingly insurmountable challenges. The essence of the feeling of *nin* during times of negative emotion is to find resolution through our endurance and perseverance in life. To persevere in the face of adversity, anger, sadness and a general feeling of overwhelming insignificance is the way to understand *nin* and your higher self. Your emotions are very powerful and can shape your present and your future. Perhaps through the path of *ninpo* or *budo* one can learn to shape their future and the present in a more positive and understanding way. Destructive emotions can erode the spirit from within. Failure to understand your emotional self can launch you into a mode whereby your life becomes a meaningless cycle of self-destruction. Unchecked, you might even extend this physical, emotional or mental abuse to those around you. There are many negative emotions that, when employed in the dojo, can be equally destructive as in other aspects of life:

- Anger
- Resentment
- Jealousy
- Hate
- Greed
- Apathy
- Grief
- Fear
- Shame
- Regret
- Hostility

Remember that emotion is energy in motion and, in the same way that we are able to manipulate energy for a higher purpose, so too can we manipulate the energy for a destructive purpose. Yet we must also face the scientific fact that energy can't be destroyed—only changed.

Persisting through Struggles

Hatsumi once said that "all struggles are temporary—a mere hurdle to circumnavigate." Yet, we always seem to give in to any struggle that we come up against. Whether it is in the dojo or in life, we always seem to take the easy way out. If one wants to learn the higher order of ninjutsu, the *budo* arts, or any martial art, one has to learn that all of the struggles we come across are temporary, but are nonetheless necessary for growth in your training and in life. If you grow spiritually, you will inevitably overcome the hurdles. However, refusal to grow may keep you rooted in the frustrating cycle that you likely find yourself in now. This cycle could be affecting anything in your life, precipitating financial hardship, relationship problems, or personal circumstances that change dramatically. Learning to endure and understanding the path that you are on is a way to achieve significant spiritual growth that will allow you to capture the essence of the beating heart of *budo*.

Struggles will present themselves for a variety of reasons. For instance, you may feel negativity and a sense of self-loathing for no clear reason, or you may be the victim of particular types of abuse at work, in your home, or even on the world wide web. Inevitably, it seems easier to give up and yet, the spirit of *nin* will keep you fighting for truth. Truth is truth no matter what, and cannot be changed—but there are those who will fail to reveal the truth through their own ignorance. This is all too prevalent in the martial arts and in life in general. This struggle within can be the ultimate expression of perseverance and endurance.

Sometimes in training we work in *mu* (empty space), seeking the weakness in an opponent and moving within a higher dimension—moving beyond material perception. Within this empty space lie the answers to all of life's questions and the path to freedom from our struggles. It is evident in one's movements where they are in their understanding of *nin* or indeed *budo* as a whole, because in the movement is the dance of material belief. The weakness that we may find is a reflection of our own, and to find the weakness in our enemies or opponents allows us to grow harmoniously and balance ourselves—thus reflecting our own perseverance and endurance by accepting our weakness and compensating for it. It must be noted, however, that weakness may not only show itself in the physical movements, but also in the intent and emotion of the individual. We must always stay in balance, for when balance is stolen or lost—we are defeated. However, the question remains: why are we defeated and in what way? The truth is that we have defeated ourselves. Seemingly, the secret is to lose balance deliberately in order to feign a weakness and so allow the seemingly defeated to become victorious. This strategy requires that we master emotion and cast off aspirations brought on by the material world. Only then can we stand in the gracious glory of victory. Beware, however; victory often breeds further hatred and contempt for the defeated. For this reason, I argue that we should show that there is no "defeat," per se—only mercy and compassion. These are the attributes of real warriorship.

Persevering through Manifestation and Intention

A truism of life is that we all want what we don't have at any given moment, and we mix up the feelings of wanting and needing, not truly understanding the difference. The *law of attraction*, which is a spiritual truth, tells us that the rate of our vibration and intention will draw to us the desire or the need or that which matches the same vibration. For instance, if you truly desire something, and you act in the belief that it is already there, your vibration—along with the universal consciousness—will bring to you what it is that you seek.

However, what many individuals miss is that not only do you have to "believe to conceive," but you must also feel the emotion that goes with it. You must first *perceive*, then *believe*, and finally *conceive*—this is the secret to manifestation. Writing daily affirmations are not enough to put the law of attraction into effect, because you're just carrying out the physical act of writing without the emotion and belief—all the necessary elements must be present for success.

The mechanism of this spiritual attraction starts with belief. Too many students fail in this belief and so find that they meet a seemingly insurmountable wall of opposition. Many years ago, when I was in the army, there was a particular wall at the confidence course that I could not get over. Each and every time I faced it, the negative emotions within me welled up like a river about to burst its banks. I did not have the belief that I could get over it, and every time I attempted it, I failed. One of my instructors told me that my problem was that I did not believe in myself, and that I should visualize easily getting over the wall. Of course, this was easier said than done, but I began to visualize myself managing to get over the wall with all my gear on. The day came when I was to face my nemesis once more. Before I began, I could see an image of myself getting over the wall. I took one long run toward it and leapt—stretching up with my hands to grab the edge. I struggled, but in my mind I held the same vision. I thought I was about to let go when, all of a sudden, I came around and found myself on the other side with the sounds of my fellow soldiers' cheering ringing in my ears. In principle, this wall was no different than the one that you face during your martial arts training in and in life—you always struggle to grab the edge and the basis of success must be belief in yourself and perseverance. Do not give up when it gets tough, for one day your wall will be scaled and defeated—even in the face of adversity.

One simple factor remains constant, and this is your intention. Hatsumi often talks about intention at length and I wonder if many people really understand what he means. How do you really describe intention? What is it, how do you feel it, and where does it come from? Intention is simply placing your awareness on a subject, movement, or desire. To hold that intention in your subconscious means that your vibration changes to match that of the intention and so activates that spiritual law of attraction. My intention was to overcome the wall and so your intention in training should be similarly focused. The purpose of wielding the power of intention should not be to show off successes, but rather to grow in our understanding of *budo* and move toward our own spiritual warriorship.

Of course, there is another facet to the utility of intention, and that is picking up the intention of others through our aura and innate psychic abilities in order to protect oneself or others from immediate danger.

To tune into someone's intention you must be able to use your psychic ability to react to their exuded energy—whether positive or negative. This is also a process of discernment and one that requires many years of training, understanding and cultivation. You can try this in the dojo but if the intention is wrong, it will not work. One cannot remain skeptical when feeling intention, as this emotion will interfere with the transference of natural universal energy that is positively or negatively charged. Try this exercise: hold your finger before you and try to feel your intent as you consciously tell your subconscious mind to bend the finger. What you're feeling is internalized power, which is universal; it is the power of your free will to choose to react to the manifested thought. Understanding just a small part of this will help you to coalesce the power within your super-conscious, thus bypassing conscious thought. In this way you can start to learn to move intuitively—without the hindrance of conscious thought. Understanding this simple process will bring you closer to enlightenment and understanding the *mu* (empty space). Working in this dimension means that you can attract all that you desire in life—but this takes perseverance and endurance. Also, working in this dimension allows you to control space between you and your opponent. Through this, one may be able to tap into the wisdom of *budo* and *nin*. Try to feel the energy that is internalized when you make a positive decision. This energy springs from intention, though you may not recognize it immediately—it may take many years of meditating before you understand the essence of your movement. If training with a weapon, *feel* the intention when you draw the weapon, and do not merely draw for the repetition of the physical movement—you must hold and internalize the power to feel its essence.

A famous statement by the swordsman Miyamoto Musashi in his *The Book of Five Rings* sheds some light on this topic:

> *The primary thing when you take a sword in your hands is your intention to cut the enemy, whatever the means. Whenever you parry, hit, spring, strike or touch the enemy's cutting sword, you must cut the enemy in the same movement. It is essential to attain this. If you think only of hitting, springing, striking or touching the enemy, you will not be able actually to cut him.*

Don't Give up on Your Training

At last we arrive at the final destination, which for some of you will be the first in your personal understanding. To endure through your training is to make small steps on your path in *budo*. I believe that Hatsumi Sensei coined this as the "beating heart of *budo*." Why beat ourselves up when we don't quite understand something or feel that we have to give up training because an injury or personal circumstance makes it harder for us? Is this enduring? No! It's giving up on life—not just the training in the dojo. Remember a true *budoka* trains every second of every hour of the day in his or her quest for enlightenment. This training does not have to consist solely of physical exercises. You can train in the martial way by just studying nature or by talking to others and putting into practice the hidden lessons that lie like jewels inside the beating heart of your own martial practice. Every day there is an opportunity to grow in mind, body and spirit. If you open your heart, you will learn. So when you have difficulty in your training, persevere and endure. Be the epitome of *nin* and realize that through your emotions, struggles and training, you have the opportunity to learn by persevering and enduring. Giving up is giving up on yourself and life—so don't! Daily appreciate the miracle that you are alive, and be grateful for it. Growing with the miracle means growing in your *budo*—for *budo* is a miracle within the universal nature that is life.

A word of caution to you students of *budo* who may face ridicule because of your faith or your beliefs: your antagonists are the ones who always rip apart your technique in order to gratify themselves. Remember that this is not about technique or indeed battle. This is about living harmoniously and learning the value of your inner spirit. Feel compassion rather than hate for your enemy, and discern who is the true warrior.

Sanshin—A Gift of Nature

At this point, you've learned a little more about our energy system and our psychic centers, and as you proceed I will add more information as necessary. Now I'll explain a little bit more about how we can comprehend this on a deeper level and blend this knowledge with a correlation to nature: this is, perhaps, the doorway to understanding nature and how, through the elements, we can develop our innate intuitive senses. I am talking about *Sanshin* or *Gogyo no Kata*.

Most who study *Sanshin* only understand its basic provision: the impression of real combat when added with other concepts such as the *Kihon Happo* (the basic eight). One of my teachers and closest friend Andrew Beattie (Shihan) once said to me that to have one without the other is meaningless, rather like eating shredded wheat cereal without the milk or sugar—it's disgusting and has no real flavor. This rings true when we look at the basics of *Sanshin no Kata*, and to understand the movements alone will give the student an appreciation for explosive moves using the legs as well as familiarity with combat techniques. The practice of *Sanshin no Kata* helps martial artists control balance, timing, and angles, as well as energy and intention. The thing is this: *Sanshin no Kata* has a much deeper meaning and a more spiritual form of direction—if you only open your heart (*kokorro*) to see it.

Sanshin, of course, is broken down to the elements of nature and five systematic techniques, which give us a sense of the energy behind it. The truth is that most of us do not make that real connection to the feeling behind *Sanshin* and its real energy. Instead we just carry out the movements without understanding what we are doing or indeed trying to achieve any growth. The five elements of *Sanshin* are *Chi* (earth), *Sui* (water), *Ka* (fire), *Fu* (wind) and *Ku* (void). I know this may sound crazy, but I often take my personal students out into the wilderness to experience what these elements of nature are while studying *Sanshin*. I get them to train in woodland areas to get the feeling of the earth and study movement of trees and near waterfalls where they will experience the essence of water and its energy and movement.

To understand fire I have students train in the presence of fire to experience the heat, explosive nature, and natural movement of the fire. For wind, I take them high in the mountains and get them to understand the energy behind wind, and the way that by the time you hear it coming, it's too late to avoid. To experience the void, I get students to understand their own intuitive mind through simple exercises that many of them are unaware they are doing while they are training—this often produces that "light bulb moment."

There is another aspect to this: through the understanding of *Sanshin* and its elements that I explained previously, we have a very real opportunity to learn to meditate and begin to develop the psychic faculties. Meditation is the first basic exercise that leads to understanding how to open up our psychic gifts. These psychic gifts are, of course, not separate from nature and so it seems fitting that we should develop them in harmony with nature in its totality.

Meditation—Before You've Gone, You're Already There

I know that when I talk of meditation, it probably conjures up an image of someone sitting in a very uncomfortable position and humming a mantra while trying to still their minds in order to reach a surreal level of enlightenment. The truth is that meditation is very simple and needs only understanding and practice to gain its benefits in a relatively short period of time. You do not have to sit for hours, days, or weeks as some teachers will tell you. In fact, you can begin to feel the benefits after only one ten-minute sitting. You probably don't realize that even in training, you are meditating: when you are performing rote movements, your conscious mind and ego are removed, and you enter a surreal, meditative space without knowing it. You can even meditate while doing *San-shin* and this is something that I encourage all of my students to do. I'll return to this topic later.

The biggest problem that most people have with meditation is overcoming laziness in order to set aside time each day to do it. Ten minutes is not a long period of time, and with a little self-discipline you'll find it easy enough to set time aside for this practice. Don't think for one minute that I am amazingly disciplined—there are times when I forget to meditate. Don't let an occasional lapse get you down. Just try to meditate as often as realistically possible, as it can take a while to learn to do properly. There is a common pitfall that you need to recognize as you begin, and I'll cover that in the following section.

Developing a Peaceful Mind

You are probably curious about what you should expect from the practice of meditation and what the difficulties may be the first few times you do it. The truth is that the problems I'm about to describe arise constantly—you just need to recognize them and let them go. For instance, most of you, when first trying out the practice of meditation, come with an expectation of having amazing ethereal epiphanies and expect to feel something quite unique or being able to instantly talk to the dead. I am sorry, but for most of you this will not happen. Very few people—other than natural mediums—ever really experience something unique or paranormal.

A great many of you will get rather annoyed as you experience the never-ending thought traffic of your mind. You may begin to get discouraged, thinking that you will never get the hang of meditation. The truth is that even the most seasoned expert in meditation has a busy mind and can't help what we call *mind chatter*.

Okay, so now you're asking, "what in God's name is 'mind chatter?'" It is really quite simple, and I will explain this by giving you a personal example. I was once in a meditation and just could not seem to settle. Every time I began to breathe deeply and concentrate on my colors or my visualization, a thought would enter my head like "*I wonder what Jo is making to eat tonight*" or "*I need to raise funds to get to Japan—what can I do... oh no, I need winter tires on the car!*" and for some reason these thoughts just kept entering my head. Every time I tried to relax myself and get back to my meditation another stray thought would jump right in there, and this was getting me down and angry. I came out of that meditation and, as usual, my wife and I got together to discuss what our guides had said to us or what we saw clairvoyantly. What had I seen? "Nothing!" I exclaimed, and I proceeded to tell her in a rather angry voice what was going on in my head, and how I felt useless. Jo then gave me the best advice ever, and I remember it to this day: "I get that too, but just let it go." I thought to myself for a moment and then waited for that "a-ha! moment"... *nothing*—not a jot, and at the time, I mentally dismissed the advice as unhelpful. That was, until the next morning when we meditated again. As I expected, I was again distracted with various thoughts. However, things were different this time! Every time a new thought would pop into my mind I would think, "*Okay, that's cool, but not now please.*" Dismissed, the intruding thoughts evaporated, and I was back into my meditation without allowing myself to be mentally derailed. No sooner had I done that, I recognized I had done exactly what my wife recommended. That's the same advice I give you all, and though it may seem inconsequential, it *is* great advice—you need to find the balance for yourself. In this way you can learn to control that mind chatter and begin to meditate so that you can experience the associated benefits.

I would now like to take you through the *Sanshin* meditation. This meditation can be done over a period of five days, and will help you achieve that awakening of the sixth dimension within your spirit.

Sanshin Meditation

This meditation will take you through five days of inner work that will help you to heal and to begin the path to psychic development within *budo* or your chosen discipline. Each day will represent one element of nature that you will meditate upon and begin to recognize its core values and lessons. The meditation will take you closer to developing that oneness with Mother Nature and to understand what *mushin* (no mind) actually means.

So to begin, you need to learn to ground yourself between the heavens and the earth and this will help to anchor your own energy to nature while removing any impurities within your *auric field*.

A Meditation Exercise to Try

This is a simple exercise that, when practiced, will only take a few moments to ground you and protect you. You should do this exercise each time before you move onto your next meditative practice.

Let's begin. Find a quiet place to sit; you can either have light music on in the background or no music at all, it depends on your preference. Ensure that the chair you sit on is comfortable and upright as this will be the best position to allow the natural breath to pass through your body—cleansing and purifying as it goes. Sit comfortably and close your eyes and begin to take deep breaths in through your nose and out through your mouth.

Begin to visualize a beautiful white light coming down from the heavens and entering the top of your head where your crown *chakra* is situated. Visualize this *chakra* as a beautiful white lily or a spinning wheel of light situated at the top of your head. See the white light moving through that *chakra* and know that it is cleansing and removing any impurities as it passes through.

Next, see the white light enter your third eye *chakra,* which is the seat of your clairvoyance and is lilac/purple in color—visualize this as a purple flower or spinning wheel of light. See that white light enter the *chakra* and see it cleanse and purify this *chakra,* removing all impurities as the white light permeates every cell of your body.

Next, the light should be moved down to the throat *chakra,* which is blue in color. Again, envision it as a flower or spinning light, and see the white light enter that *chakra* to cleanse and purify as it continues through.

Next, you will move through to the heart *chakra,* which is green or pink in color. Again, envision it as a flower or spinning light. Visualize the white pure light moving through the heart *chakra* while it cleanses and purifies.

See the white light moving into the solar plexus *chakra,* which is situated above your navel, near the center of your stomach. This is the seat and major power source of your intuition. Visualize this as a yellow flower or spinning wheel of light and see it cleanse, renew, balance and remove any negativity or impurities from the *chakra* (this is an important *chakra* to keep balanced).

The white light will now move through you and enter your sacral plexus *chakra,* which is orange in color and located just below your navel. Visualize the light cleansing the *chakra* and see it remove any impurities or negative emotions within it.

At last, the white light will move down to your root *chakra* which is red in color and situated at the very base of your spine. See it enter the *chakra* and cleanse it, visualize that white light leaving the root *chakra* and take it down through the earth and root it to the center of the earth. Visualize all the negative attachments, emotions, impurities and negative beliefs about yourself as dark specks and see them being taken into the earth to be purified.

Next, cut the chord of light and see all the negativity fall to the earth and know that your *chakra*s are now cleansed and balanced.

Finally, see the white light travel all around your body in circular fashion, creating a perfect ball of light around you—know that you are protected by your innate divinity. See the white light shoot back to the heavens above—you are now balanced as well.

Day One—*Chi* (Earth)

See yourself standing in front of a large oak door. Notice how solid this door feels and see a large gold handle on the door. Turn the handle and open the door, then walk through and ensure that the door is closed behind you. Walk forward and note that you are in the most beautiful Japanese garden, you can hear the birds singing and observe that the flowers in the garden are some of the most spectacular colors you can see. In the garden is a beautiful tree and the trunk is wide and strong. The tree has lush foliage and its roots are deeply rooted in the ground. Walk over to the tree and notice, before you, that there is a place to sit within the trunk of the tree: the tree has shaped this just for you. Sit down and feel your energy slowly merge with that of the tree's. Feel the force of the earth and nature around you, feel the span of lifetimes that the tree has been there. Notice how the tree is grounded and rooted in the earth. Feel the mighty power of the tree but also its universal beauty and energy within it. Visualize how it receives from, and gives back life to Mother Nature, and how it's a key element to your own survival. Sit for a while with this wonder of the earth and enjoy all the earthly sensations that you feel. When you are finished, make your way back through the Japanese garden and feel happy and honored that you have been here to feel the energy of Mother Nature. Walk back to the oak door at the end of the garden and walk through it making sure that you close the door behind you (this is also an element of protection). Begin to feel your body once more as you slowly wake from your relaxed state. Notice the heaviness of your muscles and feel your breath and the blood pulsing through your body. You have now completed your connection to the earth and know that you can go there at any time you desire to be in that sacred space.

Day Two—*Sui* (Water)

Water is nature's gift of life to humanity—it can be as gentle or as devastating as Mother Nature intends it to be. We need to be watered constantly in order to have optimal conditions for pure growth.

Prepare yourself in the same manner as before by cleansing and purifying through the aforementioned exercise, and once more pull the oak door and shut behind you as you enter into the Japanese garden described in the exercise for day one.

Notice that in the distance you can hear the trickling of a beautiful waterfall. Make your way to the path that leads through the garden toward the noise of the waterfall. Note the sound getting clearer as you get closer to the water and begin to feel its energy. Perceive that the little animals that are around the area have no fear of you, for they are one with nature as are you. There are butterflies that are happily flitting through the radiant flowers all around. You continue to walk through the garden, and soon you are at the edge of the waterfall. Observe how the water cascades down, turning and spinning with vibrant energy. Notice how it curls back on itself when it reaches the base, and how it evades every obstacle in its path as it flows down the river. Have an awareness of its life and death, and how gentle it can be, and how powerful the water can be. Know that you can be like the water, flowing with the rhythm of nature. See how the water does not stay still, and even when slowing to collect in a pool, the energy constantly gives life. If you try to scoop out a handful of water you find that you can't because the constant motion dissipates the water. Know that you are just like this water, and when you are content, make your way back through the garden and out toward your door. Walk through the door and close it behind you knowing that you are safe and secure. Once more feel your physical body come alive as you slowly wake from your relaxed state.

Day Three—*Ka* (Fire)

Find yourself in the garden once more and notice that in the middle of this garden is an open area that has a beautiful warming fire. Hear the crackling of the fire, and feel the warmth and the energy that the fire has to offer as you approach. Notice how it bathes area with heat and radiant light. Recognize that the warmth is life-giving and offers comfort when needed. See how life is connected by its very need to feel the comfort and solace found within the fire and within oneself See how explosive the flames can be and how they consume everything in their path. Know that you are at one with this energy and that in your heart burns the fire and passion for the universe that created you. Know that you too can be explosive and controlled. Feel the energy and realize that you are part of this energy and that you can employ its ethereal power by your own will and intention for the highest good. Know that the energy you put into your life in a positive manner will produce its rewards.

Day Four—*Fu* (Wind)

This time you find yourself at the base of a beautiful Japanese garden. You see the path that leads to the end of the garden and to a golden gate. Walk toward that gate and open it to find yourself standing at the base of a mountain with a winding golden path that follows the incline to the top. There are many animals around you. You must choose one to take along as a companion on your journey—which will you choose? Each animal is a totem and a gift from the spiritual world. As you begin your climb, you feel the sun on your face and the gentle warmth gives you a feeling of safety. Your vibrational energy will increase and you will become lighter and lighter as you ascend.

You begin to feel a gentle breeze around you and you will find it more and more comforting as you become one with this energy. Soon you will find yourself at the very top of the mountain and you feel the breeze get stronger until it is nearly strong enough to blow through you. Suddenly, like a heavenly angel, the wind picks you up and carries you along in its energy stream. You are flying high above the earth and you can see beauty all around you. You become like the wind—invisible energy that is felt but never seen. See how the trees bend and receive—they go with the flow of natural movement that is the wind's essence. Know that you are that energy and you can engage its power at any time. The wind will carry you in its ethereal gentleness back to the oak door. When you are ready, walk through and ensure that it is closed behind you. Find yourself back in your room and safely in the body.

Day Five—*Ku* (Void)

This is the final day of your meditative practice and this is when you will join all the elements of nature together into the energy that comprises your unique spirit. Find yourself at the center of the beautiful Japanese garden—see the beauty around you and notice how the tree blooms, hear the chirping of the birds around you and feel the warmth of the sun. In the distance you can hear the waterfall and you feel a gentle breeze surround you and comfort you like a loving angel's wings. Sit for a while in the middle of garden and be at one with nature. Enjoy the calmness in your soul and know that you are fully protected by your divinity and the divine spark that permeates all of nature. Know now that you are at one with all of nature and that you can employ this knowledge and energy within your training in *budo*.

What Should You Expect?

This is a five day meditation plan and guide, you should not expect too much and you should go into this knowing that the meditative practice can have dramatic effects on your mind, body and soul. If you do this properly and with conviction, you will feel calmer, you will be able to identify answers rather than continuing to futilely search for them, and you will learn the process of co-creating your destiny and manifesting your dreams and desires. In the dojo you will harness your physical energy with your own mind and body and you will begin to understand the intuitive, seamless movement that will be your new spirit.

You will be free from the chains of conscious thought and will have restricted your ego. You will sense things before they happen—as I said earlier: "Before you've gone, you're already there." A good practice to develop is to keep your journal with you and note the feelings that you get during and after your meditation. You will be able to refer back to these notes at any time to mark your progress and measure how you have grown spiritually. Take special note of how your martial practice changes. There may also be dramatic changes in your life—especially if you continue with this plan. Base your observations on a five month cycle. You will find that you are able to be happier with yourself, and more peaceful, understanding, loving, and compassionate. You may find that you understand others' points of view with more empathy and that you have a far greater level of tolerance. Whatever you find, it is all for your highest good and for the good of all humanity. I can also guarantee that you will recognize intuition more readily in your life and that you will be ready to learn to use it.

Meditating Physically with the *Sanshin Kata*

As I promised, I would like to show you how you can do the same type of meditative exercise, but instead of sitting quietly, you will be actually carrying out the *Sanshin kata* while using the technique of visualizing not only the movement but the energy felt while performing the *kata*. In the following pages I present the *Sanshin kata* taken straight from the *densho* (scroll), but after each movement I have added my own words to help explain the essence of the movement and how to join the mind and body as one.

The *Sanshin no Kata* is also known by the following names:

- *Sho shin go-kei Go-Gyo no Kata*
- *Shoshin go Gata*
- *Gako no Gata*
- *Goshin no Kata*
- *Sanshin no Tsuki*
- *Sanshin no Kata*

Remember that names are not all that important—a name will not keep you alive in the heat of the moment. You must learn to move naturally and know the basics of each movement.

What do the Names of the *Kata*s Mean?

The Earth *kata* (*Chi*) represents the most natural way to strike, with a swinging motion that becomes a form of punching that is delivered with all of your energy. This is done in much the same way as a soldier swings the arms naturally with the rhythm of the body while marching. It is also the groundwork (earth) of our *taijutsu*. Remember that the earth is the basis of who we are materially and the earth receives and gives—much in the way we receive a strike and allow ourselves to accept the energy and then give it back. This way we fear less and know that we can receive rather than block and strike with the power of nature. The Water *kata* (*Sui*), and Fire *kata* (*Ka*) are both killing strikes to the neck. The hand up (*Omote Shuto*) in *Sui* represents the raindrops that fall into the hand, from the sky to the earth. *Ka* is the light. The hand down containing the water (*Ura Shuto*), is put on the fire, putting it out (the killing strikes). The *Fu* (*Boshi Ken*) strikes to the groin affect the area of fertility, and should stop life before it begins. You must, as you strike, flow with the wind. *Ku* (sky void) uses *Chosui Dori*. This is when you must pick the flow of the timing: when to block, and when to come in. Of course, this is easier said than done, and when you begin to understand your intuitive senses you will be able to move intuitively, without conscious thought. Remember: before you've gone, you're already there! This is the epitome of intuitive movement. Imagine how advanced your martial practice will be when you can react to the conscious thought of the individual, rather than waiting for manifested movement. Think of the potential importance of this technique, and the number of applications where it would be useful. Imagine, if you will, the business director who is able to act upon a decision that *will be* made by a competitor, or the utility of being able to foresee financial events.

***Chi* (Earth)**

From *Shizen*—which is a natural posture—step back with the right foot into *Shoshin no Kamae*. Step forward with the right foot and strike with a right *San Shitan Ken*. The arm must swing from the shoulder like a pendulum. This helps you to generate natural energy. Learn to visualize each movement as a form that denotes the essence of the feeling of earth. You may wish to visualize a willow tree that receives and gives—it is rooted and bends with the rhythm of nature. Perhaps you could visualize the sun's rays as they shine down to the earth, helping to create life. You could visualize your body as roots that are deep in the ground that grow and extend to the rest of nature. As you carry out this motion, try to feel the energy in motion. Be mindful of the earth beneath your feet and realize that you live in a world of oneness—not one of duality.

***Sui* (Water)**

From left *Shoshin no Kamae,* step back and to the right with the right foot and perform a left *Jodan Uke*. Step forward with the right foot and perform a right *Omote Shuto*. Visualize a waterfall and see how the water flows down creating a circular motion that is full of power and vitality. Know that the water can give life and take life and you are free to enhance the ethereal power of the water. Know that, with the right flow and intent, you can't be held—for the water will eventually dissipate. Water is life-giving and reflects the very nature of our physical existence. It is compassionate while giving life, and resolute while taking it. In the same way, you possess natural yin and yang.

***Ka* (Fire)**

From left *Shoshin no Kamae,* step back and to the right with the right foot and perform a left *Jodan Uke.* Step forward with the right foot and perform a right *Ura Shuto.* Visualize the fire as an all-engulfing energy that is explosive in its movement. It can be warming and heartfelt or powerful and destructive. Know that with each movement you are employing the energy of fire. Perhaps you can employ this feeling in your business life, being explosive in your decision-making, not being afraid to take risks. The warmth can take the form of the heartfelt love that you show your fellow man. It can be what enables you to love unconditionally, and it can be manifested in the warmth that you show to your family. Of course, with each of these you have your balance: your destructive ability balanced with the love and control of nature—once again, an example of yin versus yang.

***Fu* (Wind)**

From left *Shoshin no Kamae,* step back and to the right with the right foot and perform a left *Gedan Uke* as you step forward with the right leg. Now step back with the left foot as you perform a right *Boshi Ken.* Visualize the power of the wind and the destructive force it can be. Notice how you don't hear it coming until it's too late to avoid it. As you move, embody the destructive force of a tornado and strike with the power of the wind behind you. Move so that "before you've gone, you're already there"—this is the power of the wind. The gentleness of wind can also be merciful and comforting when felt around you. In this way you can allow an adversary to defeat him or herself, whether in the boardroom, within familial relationships, or other external environments.

***Ku* (Void)**

From left *Shoshin no Kamae,* step back and to the right with the right foot and perform a left *Gedan Uke* (low level block) as you perform a right *Shako ken*. Then perform a right *Zenpo Geri* (front foot strike). Begin to visualize that you are at one with all of nature and within you is the energy of all the elements. See yourself as a white light that can travel and move unhindered. You can have all the power of nature at your disposal, and you know and feel all wisdom: for within that void is the energy that permeates and co-creates.

Kuji In Hand Signs

I will now discuss the reality of the *Kuji in* and dispel many myths regarding this esoteric practice. Unfortunately, Hollywood has depicted this practice as occultist, and one that will give the individual super powers or hidden supernatural abilities. However, *Kuji in* is actually a spiritual practice that was developed to enhance universal power through the focusing of intent and use of hand and finger entwining to create symbolic "seals." There are, of course, many masters out there who study this form of esotericism, and many supporting books and writings exist. It is not only the ninja who have gotten this right, for the basis of these forms are from Buddhist traditions and can be traced to eastern Asia in particular. There is so much to say about *Kuji in* that I could write an entire book about this one topic. However, for this exercise I only want to touch on the basics to give you an appreciation for this type of esotericism and its practice.

There are *mudras* (hand signs) in which interwoven fingers create geometric shapes that, when used with the sounds of the mantras, will catapult the user into a transcendental state and open the nine innate energy gateways. However, my experience has been that one can achieve the same with just a few minutes of meditation—how else would I be able to connect with the spiritual world in order to pass on messages of life after death, love and hope? But for some, the *Kuji in* is a necessary practice to help them work with energy and enter transcendental meditative states of consciousness.

As a matter of fact, the *Kuji in* will open up your innate psychic abilities through its meditative states, which are essentially no different from the type of meditative practices described earlier in this book. Most *budo* masters have opened up these psychic gateways—either through *Kuji in* practice or meditation and practice of the martial ways—and some don't even recognize it! I know from personal experience that Hatsumi is very psychic, but I believe his aptitude has nothing to do with the *Kuji in*, but is rather attributable to the innate spirituality that he has. As for me, I enter the transcendental state naturally, without the *Kuji in*, and my goal is to teach you how to do it too. However, I'm not advocating that you forsake *Kuji in* practice. Everything has a place. For instance; the practice can reduce the problems with discursive thought processes. If it works for you, then so be it.

I'm not going to attempt to teach you how to use the *Kuji in* in this book, for it takes many years of practice and understanding to master, and many other books are dedicated to this one subject. A great place to start is with François Lépine, who has published many works on this subject, or fellow *buyu* (Bujinkan group of "warrior friends") Dr. James Clum, whose self-published work is most excellent. There are nine symbols—which are also known as the *gateways of power*—

and each has its own meaning. The number nine symbolizes completion in the Buddhist system. Each symbol consists of a *mudra* (movement), *mantra* (sound) and *mandalla* (thought). The nine are as follows:

Rin Reinforces the physical and mental aspects of the energy of the self.

Kyo Increases the flow of energy and mastery of the *energy body* (aura).

Toh Enhances the universal relationship, creating harmony and balance.

Sha Speeds healing and regeneration of the body on both levels: spiritually and physically.

Kai Develops premonition and intuition, and enhances the ability to feel the energy body.

Jin Promotes telepathy, communication, and inner knowledge, i.e. clairaudience.

Retsu Enhances perception and mastery of space and time dimensions (clairvoyance).

Zai Fosters your relationship with nature.

Zen Brings enlightenment.

The key to using these nine symbols, and possibly the only constant, is that you need to employ varying degrees of intention in order to activate them. In order to achieve the desired state of mind you must effectively produce the necessary visualization, intention, emotion, and belief. Doesn't this sound familiar? Identical prerequisites will bring the same benefits through meditation, without all the "pomp and circumstance" involved with *Kuji in*. It has also been said that the *Kuji in* is a meditative practice, but viewed through my professional understanding of meditation, I'm not sure that I completely agree. To me, the *Kuji in* is a way to focus spiritual efforts and a form of "switch" that allows one to meditate or activate hidden energy channels within oneself. However, the meditative quality of *Kuji in* is open to individual interpretation, and there is no right or wrong answer.

In practice, the *mudras* are intertwined to create a shapes that have meaning and symbolic intention. What you may not know is that the intertwining of the fingers also activates certain meridian points in the body, which are energy channels—rather like your *chakra*s. This energy dances together with the *chakra*s to create the link, and bond with the higher realms of consciousness. These higher realms of consciousness have a direct correlation to your *chakra*s and energy body, which are your gateways to the spirit world and form your natural interconnection to the universe.

Kuji Kiri Symbolic Cuts

You may have seen this being practiced when Hatsumi Sensei "cuts" symbols in the air with his fingers. It's also present in almost every ninja film going: they make the cuts and then seem to gain mystical powers. Why do we cut? *Kuji Kiri* literally translates as "nine symbolic cuts." These motions invoke the installation of nine energy systems (or seals) that, when activated, help to empower the user. Just as the energy from the intent is placed on the seal in *Kuji in,* this same sense of intention is brought to bear when cutting the *Kuji Kiri* in order to use seals for healing and gaining insight. In short, the *Kuji Kiri* is the communication or link between the universe and your higher consciousness. This is not just used by the ninja—many monks, priests, and practitioners from other religions and arts use the nine symbolic cuts. As a *reiki* (Japanese healing art) master, I am often cutting the *reiki* symbols to activate this intention or the power of the *reiki* seals. It must be noted that the founder of *reiki,* Dr. Usui, was in fact a master of many *budo* arts. These symbolic cuts help create mental focus, and activate that intention behind the physical act. It's rather like telling your mind, "*Okay, I'm ready to meditate. You must quiet the conscious side of me so that I can gain access to, and control of my higher self for the betterment of me or whomever I am serving at this time for the highest good.*" In this way you can spiritually and physically express your intention and create a sacred space for yourself so that you can move into that transcendental state of super consciousness.

As you can see, there is nothing really mystical about the *Kuji Kiri*. It's not a necessary practice when you can achieve the same results by using your intuition or natural psychic ability and your own simple ten-minutes-a-day meditative practice.

THE THIRD RING

Psychic Development and its Role in *Budo*

"A respected Buddhist scholar once said; 'Archery is, therefore, not practiced solely for hitting the target; the swordsman does not wield the sword just for the sake of outdoing his opponent; the dancer does not dance just to perform certain rhythmical movements of the body. The mind has first to be tuned to the unconscious.' "

—D.T. Suzuki

Why Develop?

Yes, I know what you're thinking (I'm psychic!). All joking aside, you're probably wondering, "why should I develop psychic abilities?" The truth is that most of you have a certain image of what a psychic medium, a fortune-teller, or a seer is. I would be willing to bet that your impression is inaccurate. At the outset you probably don't really grasp the scope of the divine power that we all hold within ourselves, or the way divine providence has played a role in putting this book into your hands.

Some of you have undoubtedly conjured up an image of an elderly wise-person sitting with a mystical crystal ball, Tarot cards, or even gazing into the water. Let me enlighten you: I am very spiritual, extremely psychic and mediumistic, and definitely no angel—nor do I stare into crystal balls or the like. I'm a normal guy you'd pass on the street without a second thought, and to look at me you would not begin to suspect my psychic abilities.

Imagine if you could enhance the power that you hold within your hands, that you could manifest a happier life. I am sure that as a business executive you could see the advantages in being able to make well-placed executive decisions in the boardroom. You could intuitively know if you should do business with a customer or a colleague just by using your intuition, or you may have an intuitive feeling about what is happing within the markets. The truth is that developing your intuitive side within the dojo can enhance your life in all directions—and you don't have to sit in what we in my line of work call a "development circle."

We all develop for different reasons, and some individuals develop purely to indulge their egos and the desire for some form of fame or fortune. Others will develop their intuitive senses because they have experienced some kind of paranormal event and some will develop just out of curiosity. Why should we develop these senses in the martial arts? Allow me to give you a hypothetical situation. Imagine that you are faced by an attacker on the street who may be wielding a dangerous weapon with the intent to rob you, or worse—kill you and perhaps your partner too, should you be with one. Now as an individual, you have been studying the martial arts for many years and may have even cross-trained in other arts. You have studied the *densho* or the syllabus of your chosen style, and through all of that hard study, you are able to rattle off the names of every technique in there. You are able to demonstrate the techniques and no doubt you are also competent in teaching those techniques to others. Perhaps you have your own dojo and teach classes regularly. Now, imagine that this attacker lunges at you with all his available force, and then his friends join in as well. The energy is aggressive, and fists, legs, and bodies fly at you from everywhere. Your mind is turning upside down and you feel a flurry of punches and kicks land on you, causing extreme pain. You don't know where to turn, and in desperation, you try to recall those techniques buried deep in your conscious mind as you make the decision to try to fight back. But no matter how much you try, you don't seem to be making any progress—that's when the blood from your cut eyebrow blinds you. All hope is lost. You and your partner are violently thrown to the ground causing further injury. You lie there in immense pain. You can't understand where that pain has come from—the beating felt so different from even the most punishing sparring session experienced in the dojo. There is a constant pain from your side and everything feels wet. To your horror, you discover that your shirt is soaked through with blood, and you realize that you have been stabbed in the throes of the assault. The shock runs through your body and your heart is racing. Time seems to slow as your vision dims to black, and the last thing you hear is the sound of the sirens.

I realize that this scenario is pretty gruesome, and is obviously not the sort of thing that you ever want to face. There is, however, an amazing power within you that could save your life and that of your partner's. It's innate and is buried deeply within us all. We humans have a survival instinct that seems to spring from nowhere when necessary. Thus, some individuals are able to survive some of the most treacherous conditions known to man, whether it be the result of kidnapping, terrorism, or just finding yourself in a position where you are stranded and have to survive in a vast and dangerous wilderness. However, here is the paradox: most of us will deny and withhold that survival instinct—even at the risk of becoming "just another statistic."

I recently received a phone call from a young man who was a *dan* grade (black belt) in taekwondo and had studied for a long time. He told me that over the holidays he found himself the victim of a serious unprovoked attack. He also proclaimed that he was so surprised that in all his years of training, he was unable to defend himself during the attack. No matter what he did, he could not outwit or fight his attackers with what he knew. He said, "Jock, I received the beating of my life and could not defend myself—even as a black belt." My friends, the truth is that no matter how much you may study and practice the fundamental facets of the art you study, you may never be able to seriously defend yourself. This is the reason why you should develop your intuitive senses and natural psychic ability through the study of *budo* or your chosen martial art, by opening your spirit to real spirituality, which is not found in religious belief. Allow me to explain that statement. I have discussed your natural survival instinct, which is primal and a natural part of our being. As violent attacks come to you, your natural intuition will have a way of moving you out of danger, for as you train all of the senses and your mind, body and soul, you will be able to detect and recognize subtle changes in energy. This form of perception is far more extensive than you could even imagine and is beyond your physical senses. With training, all the senses will work together as one spiritual unit. I can't tell you when you will achieve this enlightenment because it is beyond conscious perception, but you will know when it happens. This is perhaps what Hatsumi Sensei is talking about when he explains about working in a higher dimension.

The *Godan* Test

There is a test in the Bujinkan that you take to pass *Godan* (fifth *dan*); it is known by many other names, one of which is *Saaki*—not the kind you drink, just in case you're wondering. As there is so much conjecture surrounding the history of the test, I will only theorize about how it works.

The test involves a *shihan* (chosen by Dr. Hatsumi) and a student. The chosen *shihan* will stand behind the student while the student kneels in the other direction—unable to see to the cutter behind him. The person administering the cut with the *bokken* (a wooden or bamboo practice sword) will do so at an appropriate juncture when the *shihan* feels he has mustered the real killing intent from within. The student being tested must be able to intuitively sense the formation of killing intent behind him in order to dodge at the appropriate moment.

When I took the test, I was fortunate enough to have sat under the guidance of several people, who were also present. Duncan, one of the Australian *shihan* training in Japan was asked to deliver the testing cut, and following some teaching and discussion of the test to those above my grade, I was given the chance to sit for the test, and following two practice cuts with the *bokken* where I fell into "the feeling" I finally submitted to the tug of my body's innate intuition to get me out of the way. To try to put this into more understandable terms, I have asked Andrew—also an Australian *shihan*, and one who has kicked my sorry butt into finding a way to step up my *taijutsu* "game"—to add his thoughts to explain the idea of *Saaki* and the *Godan* test:

> *The Bujinkan is a place for one to try to recognize the laws of nature, the truth about human nature, and to be able to cut through illusion—not to simply*

understand tricks, but to see the truth: about a person, a situation, or the whole of what we are part of. To study the martial arts is to attempt to humble oneself in order to gain knowledge of one's ability, spirit / heart, and overall capacity. To understand budo, *or* "bushido"*—the warrior's path, unique and difficult as it is—is to unite these aspects in order to master your own self and accept and understand what it means to live on the "sword's edge" between life and death.*

The Saaki *in the Bujinkan is neither a test of one's technical ability or knowledge. That responsibility belongs to those teaching you, and to you to ensure that the knowledge of your* taijutsu *is not ego driven or that your physical abilities are not lacking or inferior due to laziness. Do not calibrate your expectations based on "time served"—this part of your training requires sustained effort over years! The purpose of the test is to awaken the student to instinct and the operation of the natural world. It is a beginning, in training, to understand that trust in our instinct and "feeling" is the way of true survival, both morally and physically.*

Passing the test itself shouldn't be looked upon as an achievement, rather, as a humbling step, because in passing Godan *your own mortality is raised for consideration: the test serves as a mirror held up to give you insight into your position in the "universe."*

Ranking in the Bujinkan and in other budo *arts sometimes occurs before the necessary skill for that rank is attained. This is why the taking of the test should be a humbling experience—because it defines the beginning of* mushin, *where your* taijutsu *begins to explore itself.*

Jock, of all people, knows that I speak the truth, that I value training, skill and real ability—not self-serving boastfulness. Trust me, there's enough of that in the world already. As my teachers in budo *have done for me, I too try to instill the importance of this understanding and have hammered this home to Jock. I also believe that we are part of something greater, and that there are reckonings beyond the five senses. As* "Shinobi no mono," *we should seriously consider what we learn at* Godan, *and always question the perceived, to lift any fog, or hidden veil in our journey to discover truth. In this manner—with understanding, a good heart, and humility—you will find real understanding of* budo.

— Andrew Beattie,
Shihan (FuDan), Bujinkan Dojo Shihan

My Views on *Godan*

I am aware that many individuals have their own views on the *Godan* test and no doubt have drained many a beer discussing how good or bad the test was for someone, and who should or should not have passed the test. I have listened to these conversations and tried to add my own two cents-worth from time to time—but my thoughts are often wasted on deaf ears. Others always think they know best and will often judge without due consideration and understanding. At the end of the day, we have no say in who passes or fails and only Soke has the final casting vote.

What I am about to share with you comprises my views on the *Godan* test and I know that I will upset some and some others may agree with me. I am not looking for everyone to agree, as sometimes we need to have differing views to continue our growth. My views are based on my experience as a professional psychic medium and one who understands the spiritual world more than most. You will remember that I said that Soke was an incredibly intuitive and psychic individual. He has an awareness of people that I have never seen before and is able to tune into the *kokorro* (heart) of the individual. However you must also be aware that he is not godlike and is very much human, therefore he is not above making rash judgements or making wrong choices. We must be careful not to worship, but to learn from him as a teacher and master of the arts. Nevertheless, his psychic ability does impress me and I know that even he does not think it is psychic. Perhaps one day I will get the opportunity to discuss this with him if not now on the earthly plane, then most certainly when he passes—though I hope that is not anytime soon.

The Pathway of Intent

I want to discuss the *intent* that we have been talking about, and I will use a few illustrations. First of all, intention is around us every day of our lives, and we probably use that intention several hundred or perhaps even thousands of times a day without knowing it or even perceiving that it exists. Imagine that you are sitting in your chair and in your mind a thought comes to you to have a cup of coffee. You then decide that you will have to make that cup of coffee, but in order to do this you will have to stand up. Suddenly your muscles begin to contract and move according to the thought pathway that determined your movement. Now, to understand that pathway and that intent, you need to be able to recognize the change in universal energy around you, and that will be felt in your own energy body and through the *chakra* system. You will not be able to do that immediately, but I hope that persevering through this book's training will help you to recognize that feeling.

Russell Targ states that, "although each of us obviously inhabits a separate physical body, the laboratory data from a hundred years of parapsychology research strongly indicate that there is no separation in consciousness."

The above statement is very profound, but it's basically just describing how we are all part of the natural energy that permeates everything and manifests all that is in the world or indeed the universe. Thus, the first step to learning to recognize and feel the energy around you is to admit to yourself that you are one with the universe and do not live in a world of duality.

So how does this correlate to ascertaining intent during the *Godan* test? Well, I have a theory that I call "*the pathway of intent*," and this is the same pathway that I teach my students no matter what level they've achieved. Understanding this pathway will help you tune into the energy around you.

I'll present what occurs during the administration of a typical test in order to explain the mechanism of intent from a spiritual and psychic point of view. I'll showcase some of my own feelings as part of this discussion, but it must be understood that this is my perception, which may be different from yours. However, this information is presented to help you understand the pathway of intent.

During the administration of the *Godan* test, a chosen *shihan* will be behind the student who is to be tested. Normally, the student will feel somewhat nervous. Prior to my test, my feeling was that I had to go within to open up my own energy or aura. This may be the same impression given to others as well. As the *shihan* stands behind; he begins to build up the intention by visualizing an act of aggression toward the student—on this point I've had to make an assumption, as I don't know what goes on in the mind of each individual *shihan*. This becomes a negative thought form that will build in the auric field and will be sent through the telepathic channels—which at this time will have overlapped with one another. If the intent or the thought form does not magnetically attract but rather repels,* the individual taking the test will (hopefully) recognize this within the energy field on a higher spiritual level and evade. This evasion is not done on a conscious level but rather on a spiritual level. This evasion is the manifestation of a natural, intuitive will to survive against all odds, and it comes from the spirit within (the psyche). You now have my theory of the intent pathway, which may cover some distance in the quest to understand how we react to intention.

This type of intuitive intention is also evident in the animal kingdom. The famed biologist Rupert Sheldrake wrote about this in his book: *The Sense of Being Stared At*. "The most obvious possibility is that it evolved in the context of predator–prey relations. Prey animals that could detect when predators were looking at them would probably stand a better chance of surviving than those that could not."†

In the purview of the ninja there is great emphasis on the natural world and the animal kingdom. This is also evident in elements of traditional kung fu. We can learn so much from the animal kingdom—it is a great teacher. Try this exercise the next time you are in the countryside or even sitting in your home and watching the little birds feeding in your garden. Stare at the bird intently and then, when you're ready, begin to visualize a scene in which you are picking up a gun and aiming it at the bird. Believe that you are going to kill the bird. If you manage to encapsulate the real feeling, then the bird will feel the negative energy and evade—making its escape.

---

* This is due to the positively charged negative energy that is not a vibrational match.

† From *The Sense of Being Stared At by Rupert* Sheldrake. Three Rivers Press, 2004.

Hatsumi alludes to this intent in the book: *Essence of Ninjutsu*:

> *Let me tell you briefly how the* Godan *test is done: A judge holds up a sword. An examinee sits in front of him with his back to the judge. The judge utters a few words to mark the start and cuts unexpectedly at the trainee's head. The trainee must dodge it in a fraction of a second. According to [a certain] photographer, if you aim your camera at [...] a horse [he] is so conscious of being watched that he will never give you a chance for a good shot.*‡

Exercise: *Shuriken* Intent

It's time to try a little exercise that I have devised. I call this the *shuriken intent exercise*. Select a training *shuriken* (or a real *shuriken* if you have a properly set up target area). Now, in order not to make this seem too "new-agey," you are going to have some fun with the exercise. I don't expect you to hit the target every time—or at all, frankly. What I want you to gain from this is the ability to identify the feeling of your own decisive intent.

You must set up your area and make sure that everything around you is safe, and that you are able to sit in total silence. Make sure no one will disturb you. If you are working with a partner, ensure that they remain silent. What you need to do is try to meditate for a few moments or just enjoy sitting in silence while you try to quiet your mind. Don't worry if random thoughts enter your mind, the trick is to notice them and just allow them to leave as naturally as they came in. Sit like this for ten minutes or so and try to breathe in and out as deeply

‡ From *Essence of Ninjutsu* by Masaaki Hatsumi. McGraw-Hill, 1988.

and rhythmically as possible. Now, get your partner to blindfold you and sit a short distance away from your target. As your mind returns to quietness, raise your hand into a position that will allow you to release the weapon toward the target, and continually focus in on that quiet time in your own space. When you feel that you are ready, create the intent and thought process necessary to throw the *shuriken* toward the target. Don't worry if you don't hit anything—instead; notice the feeling in your body: did anything feel different? Are there any changes in the energy around you? If so, you must learn to recognize that same feeling time and time again; each time you create the same intent. If you have felt subtle changes around you, then you have identified basic intention. From here you can develop your sensitivity to be able to feel subtle changes in energy fields.

The Subconscious Responds to Intent

As I've mentioned, I coined the phrase "before you've gone, you're already there" and I want to explain a little more about what it means. The essence of this statement is my belief about how we use our intuitive senses in the dojo or while defending ourselves against a violent attack, or indeed: for prevention before an attack occurs.

When we train in the dojo, we train to get better, quicker, fitter, and to learn to move our bodies in ways above and beyond their presupposed capabilities. What you may not realize is that you are learning to "become one" with your physical body. If you recognize the simple truth that you are one with all of nature, you will soon begin to enter the sixth dimension—and your body will react accordingly. One forges the spirit within the dojo, and that spirit will undoubtedly be the key to unlocking the door to the higher self. You would be forgiven for thinking that we are seeking to develop altered states of consciousness; however, that certainly isn't true, for you are part of the one consciousness that permeates all things. You are part of the divine creating force, and therefore have nothing to fear but fear itself. There is no way to become separate from that force, and therefore there is nothing "altered" in any state we choose to move into—it is only a different expression of the same consciousness. Any individual who persists in the belief that there are separate states of consciousness has, in fact, isolated himself or herself from nature, and therefore does not know the secrets of the real martial arts.

When we are at one with this consciousness, we begin to feel the subtle imbalances in energy and in nature around us. When we face an opponent or when we are close to them—whether it be in training or during a confrontation—we can feel the slight changes in an opponent's balance and we can detect their emotional state with our higher self, which will give us that essential edge. In the dojo, the ability to detect subtle energy variations helps us to re-train our bodies to work in tune with our energy. The upshot of all of this is that we can then detect the intent of an opponent before they have moved to carry out their physical act of aggression. We can also detect the openings and weaknesses in our own movement and close them off intuitively or exploit the weaknesses of an opponent. Perhaps this is what people consider to be "ninja mind control," yet the truth is there is nothing specifically "ninja" about it—it is prevalent in all martial arts that teach the value of a correct heart and the forging of the spirit.

Anger and aggression will subdue the psyche and render you unable to feel the emotion and the energy around you. Therefore, when someone launches an attack your intuition will be muffled—as if you have become deaf and blind. Before you know it, the attack will be underway, leaving you little time to react. You must learn to react *subconsciously* rather than with relatively plodding conscious thought. It is not enough to think where a hand or foot has to be placed in order to move through the motions to complete the cycle of a technique. By the time that thought has arrived in your conscious mind, you may be eating dirt, or worse still—dead.

The very physical aspect of training, together with the forging and fortifying of the internal spirit will naturally open the psychic senses to enable intent-detection and self-protection. An old *budo* master (as written in *kenjutsu*'s *Gekken Sodai*) was sitting in his garden meditating and enjoying his own space as he did each morning. Suddenly and without any thought (intuitively), he jumped up as if there was immediate danger in his vicinity and began to scan the vicinity. Looking around, he could find nothing and became rather perplexed trying to reconcile how he felt with the apparent absence of danger. He knew, through his training, that he was able to sense danger around him. After returning to the dojo he started recounting this story to his students. As he was talking, his senior student walked forward, looking rather embarrassed and humbled. The student explained that while the master was in the garden meditating, he'd dropped by to visit. When he spied his master in such a defenseless posture, he imagined how easy it would be to sneak up on him and attack him. It was at this point that the master reacted and the student, unnerved, ran off.

There is a kung fu style that promotes spiritual development in order to free the mind of rational thought. The spirit moves unhindered with the beauty of the rhythm of nature. This is exactly the same feeling that we try to get in the Bujinkan; to move with unhindered subconscious impulse, free from rational thinking. In this way we are able to move into the dimension that Soke so often speaks about, though so many fail to grasp. The training in the Bujinkan is indeed intuitively-oriented, and my saying "before you've gone, you're already there" is evocative of our work in the sixth dimension: learning to flow without the restrictions of the ego and perceive with the heart rather than the physical eyes in our heads.

The Fourth Ring

Developing Your Psychic Ability

> *"Today [marks] eighteen years since Takamatsu passed away. I often talk with him in heaven while giving lessons to my students, wet with perspiration. The conversation between us goes on secretly and soundlessly. I continue this with all my heart and mind."**
>
> —Hatsumi M.

The quotation above epitomizes the mediumistic quality of our Soke, and whether or not you believe in mediumship, he obviously *does*, and takes part in "the walk in the garden of the spirit." One day, I will hold this conversation with him and his ancestors. Interestingly, I picked up certain things while I was in the *hombu* ("headquarters" dojo) in Noda, Japan—I heard the voices of individuals who had passed. But that's a story for another time.

Before we move on to the development of psychic ability, you must learn what the various aspects of these gifts are.

* From *Essence of Ninjutsu* by Masaaki Hatsumi. McGraw-Hill, 1988.

There are many gifts and some people will be stronger in one than another. We will look at the general methods of development and how these may be employed in the dojo. First, you must understand that we have to learn the language of the soul, which is the main method of communication that I use when I give one-to-one readings for my clients. This language can't really be given a definitive label. As Hatsumi says, most of it goes on in silence and in the void. Don't think that as you develop, you will start to see visions or have major epiphanies while training. For the most part, you will be "consciously unaware" that you are using these gifts, and your inner power will become your main driving force rather than your rational mindset.

A Word of Caution

Another point you should take into consideration is that you have to protect yourself at all times by using the little exercise with the *chakras* described earlier on page 52. In addition to the exercise, you can just ask for protection or visualize white light surrounding you. As with every other aspect of life, there are spiritual dangers to be avoided, and developing your sensitivities to the other realms is no different. This practice is very dangerous if not done properly and with the correct intent. This is not something to enter into lightly—there are wandering spirits that will latch onto your aura to play havoc with your mind and body if the opportunity presents itself.

The primary gifts of the soul are as follows:

- Clairvoyance
- Clairaudience
- Clairsentience
- Claircognizance

What Is Clairvoyance?

This gift is the ability to see the world of the spirit and to receive images from the void. There are two methods of clairvoyance. There is *subjective clairvoyance* in which the individual perceives the images in the mind's eye (which is known as the *third eye chakra*). Most individuals use this form of clairvoyance and everyone has the ability to awaken this dormant gift. There is the second type of clairvoyance, which is *objective clairvoyance,* and that is the ability to perceive images and the world of spirit outside of yourself through your physical eyes. Many psychic mediums claim this when they are giving readings and I have to say, it irks me. I'm sure you know the ones I'm talking about! They tell you that your father, mother or someone who has passed to spirit is standing next to you and then fail to give you accurate information regarding the aesthetic state of the individual or what they are saying. The truth is that they see subjectively. However, there are those who *can* perceive outside of themselves; I am one of those but I have to admit that the times that I do objectively see are few and far between—it is the spirit world that controls this. I suppose I should count myself fortunate in this—I practically soil myself every time it happens, and my heart feels like it's going to burst from my body!

I am convinced that Hatsumi and other great masters are able to perceive clairvoyance, though I can't be sure about this until I get a chance to discuss it with them. The Aikido founder Morihei Ueshiba had the ability to clairvoyantly see objectively. When asked how he was able to avoid being hit by an attacker wielding a sword, he remarked:

> *It was nothing, just a clarity of mind and body. When the opponent attacked, I could see a flash of white light—the size of a pebble, flying before the sword.*

> *I could see clearly that when a white light gleamed, the sword would follow immediately. All I did was avoid the streams of white light.**

This is an example of the master's ability to perceive objectively—the light that preceded the blow. Now, I am not saying that you will be able to do this with just a little meditative practice, and I must inform you that it takes many years of painstaking development and devotion to the task to be able to do it effectively. Most of you will not reach this level, but some may—with the right forging and adjoining of mind, body and soul. This type of objective perception is what we must strive to achieve in due time, and is exactly what Hatsumi is referring to when he talks about perceiving the invisible.

What Is Clairaudience?

This is probably one of the most misunderstood gifts of the spirit. The ability to hear spiritual messages both objectively and subjectively is the gift of *clairaudience.* This is normally silent dialogue that goes on in the mind of the medium when working subjectively. It is the ability to perceive words in the void in your own language that you can understand. As with clairvoyance, there is the contrasting part of the gift that allows you to hear clearly with your own physical ears. Believe me, if and when this happens to you, it will frighten the proverbial crap out of you! It most certainly had this effect on me.

If you are reading this in silence you will hear the words being imprinted in your conscious mind as you follow each word, and this is a clairaudience of sorts. However, when you hear the same type of dialogue in your mind but the words

---

* From *On the Warrior's Path* by Daniele Bolelli. Blue Snake Books, 2008.

come to you out of the blue to warn you or tell you something—*that's* true clairaudience. When your conscious mind is focused on something completely different, and the mental voice breaks in unbidden, this is clairaudience of a *subjective* nature. I refer you once again to Papasan's (Ed Martin's) little story in which he heard the warnings (page 18)—this, of course, was a form of clairaudience.

Another example of this type of clairaudience was recounted to me by one of my students, who was in a town after dark, walking home from work. He usually took the same route, and was also accustomed to listening to music on his iPod as he walked. On this particular occasion however, he had a pervasive sense of foreboding, and presently he heard a voice in his mind clearly telling him not to walk the usual route and to deviate at once. He was so startled to hear this voice in his head over the music he was playing that he immediately took heed. I am sorry to say that on the same evening, and at that particular time, another young man was stabbed by two youths who were out looking for trouble along my student's usual route. The gift of clairaudience stopped my student from becoming a violent crime statistic. You can clearly deduce from this that he heard the warning subjectively, which more than likely saved his life.

The famed medium Doris Stokes could hear the voices of spirit clearly and using her physical ears—*objective clairaudience*. She had the ability to pass on amazingly accurate messages from the spirit world because of the clarity. During one of my own seminars, I heard the voice of an older woman tell me her name and that her grandson was attending whom she wished to speak to. This voice was not from within and I heard the sound clearly, in the same way I would have heard while speaking to a colleague.

What Is Clairsentience?

This is the ability to feel spirit or to feel conditions of energy that surround you. This is felt within your body and on a physical level. To give you an example of this type of feeling I will recount one of my own experiences. During a class one evening my eyes were fixated on this particular student, and every time I looked at him I felt physically sick and dizzy. I asked to see him in the back room and when I went inside I heard a name being called to me. I was immediately aware of the spiritual presence of a person who had tragically passed. It was the brother of the student who stood before me. I felt like I could not breathe and was practically gasping for breath. I then felt a physical rope being put around my neck and I knew beyond a shadow of doubt that his brother had passed by suicide. I conveyed this information to the student in question and he confirmed that is was true. This is an example of how we, as mediums, are able to perceive feelings and conditions of the spirit world. The student in question felt like a weight had been lifted from him and no sooner had this been done than he began to work above and beyond his preconceived notion of the limits of his physical capabilities in the dojo. Things came easier and he began to move more skillfully. Sometimes we even erect our own barriers because of emotional turmoil that we have experienced but haven't released. It feels rather like a pillow muting the sound of something—you know you've heard something, but you can't hear it clearly. Once these barriers have been smashed through, your training becomes more productive and you suddenly get that "a-ha! moment" that your instructor is probably always talking about.

What Is Claircognizance?

This is probably the main psychic sense that you will use within your chosen art or your understanding of *budo*. However, this sense may go unnoticed for a very long time. In essence, this is the highest form of knowing, and it will be the sense that will keep you alive in the heat of an attack or indeed spur you to take critical preventative measures. It's the amalgamation of mind, body and spirit as one complete unit; as a potential violent attack comes toward you, your body will move unconsciously and intuitively. Your natural will to stay alive in the face of danger will automatically engage, just like the working of your autonomic nervous system—It will happen and you won't know it. To explain how this relates to my own profession, claircognizance provides a medium with the ability to know exactly what to say without employing conscious thought. In his book, *The Warriors Path*, Daniel Bolleli alludes to this when he describes how his training allows him to ascertain someone's true character simply by looking into his or her eyes for a few moments—an assessment that might take someone else a number of years to determine. This is claircognizance at work. Within the dojo when training, or perhaps doing *randori*—a free-form style of light sparring that helps to develop natural movement. This type of knowing will allow your body to move intuitively without the need for conscious thought, and will help to free your mind from the bondage of material thought.

In this chapter, I have only discussed the gifts that I feel pertain to our training in *budo*. These gifts help us unify all of our five senses as well as our sixth sense into one spiritual unit that can be used not only in training, but in all aspects of your life. However, there are two other sensate gifts that are certainly available, and these are *clairalience* (smelling) and *clairgustance* (tasting). However, I don't believe that the development of these abilities is necessary for your martial arts training.

Scientific Basis for the Sixth Sense

No book on psychic abilities would be complete without references to positive proof from the scientific community that bolsters the claims that the sixth sense exists. I could write another volume that only presents the evidence for the sixth sense, but the overwhelming amount of detail would bore some of you and detract from the overall message that I want to get across. However, I'd like to cite a few details regarding the science and the pioneers in the field, and I urge you to look these up for yourself to increase your understanding. I also know some of you will be hardened skeptics and possibly followers of the noted skeptic James Randi. The thing you must realize is that if you do not want to accept evidence—no matter how strong—then you will never accept it, even if a spirit manifests right in front of you. Deep down, I believe this denial comes from an internal fear of things that can't be perceived with the material eyes, or a fear of the unknown. However, sight alone does not rationalize some commonly accepted beliefs. Consider the following example: you are convinced of the reality of the air that you breath—yet you can't see it, grasp it or indeed quantify it, as it is intangible. You believe that we are all made of energy and that our composite, vibrating atoms about bound up in molecules and cells that give the illusion of the solidity through which we all partake in the greater scheme of things.

Lynne McTaggart writes, "Our natural state of being is in relationship, a tango, a constant state of one influencing the other. Just as the subatomic particles that compose us cannot be separated from the space and particles surrounding them, so living beings cannot be isolated from each other... By the act of observation and intention, we have the ability to extend a kind of super-radiance to the world."*

Without the air, we have no life. We know that air can be broken down into its constituent elements, yet we still fail to see it—though we can feel its effects and therefore we have no choice but to accept its existence. Most of us believe in a supreme being or a force that is divinity in action. Through this belief, we demonstrate faith, because we can't perceive divinity with our own physical eyes. Perhaps we even see the effects of this or feel the effects via some miracle or event that cannot be explained by science alone. Some individuals will always choose not to believe because they do not want to turn their already scientifically-organized world upside down—and that is fine with me. But what I hope to achieve is to give you some idea that there are other possibilities all around us, and these are only a few of the possibilities that we can investigate. Why do we need to know *how* it works? Isn't it enough to see the energy in action when it unquestionably brings great benefit to all of humanity? Noted German physicist Max Planck once said:

> *Modern physics has taught us that the nature of any system cannot be discovered by dividing it into its component parts and studying each part by itself... We must keep our attention fixed on the whole and on the interconnection between the parts. The same is true of our intellectual life. It is impossible to make a clear cut between science, religion, and art. The whole is never equal simply to the sum of its various parts.*

---

* From *The Field* by Lynne McTaggart. HarperCollins Publishers, 2003.

There have been many fine scientists who have expanded the boundaries of science and challenged age-old beliefs while offering new hypothesis and new quantifiable beliefs.

Russell Targ* is a physicist and author who was a pioneer in the development of the laser and laser applications, and was co-founder of the Stanford Research Institute's investigation into psychic abilities in the 1970s and 1980s for the American Military and the Intelligence community. This work continues to this day with my good friend Dale Graaf. Though perhaps not supported by the government, he continues with this work and I keep close dialogue with him—we're hoping to continue with these experiments that connect our requisite fields. This previously classified work, concerning what is now widely known as *remote viewing,* was published in *Nature,* the *Proceedings of the Institute of Electrical and Electronics Engineers (IEEE),* and the *Proceedings of the American Association for the Advancement of Science.* He is the author of many books and has co-authored eight books dealing with subjects such as the scientific investigation of psychic abilities, Buddhism, and a recent autobiography. He now pursues ESP research in Palo Alto, California, and often appears at scientific and paranormal conferences to talk about the work. In so doing, he and Dale keep the science alive. The following example of the ESP evidence that he arranged is from a secret Soviet site. It shows remote viewing—the ability to perceive accurate information and images that are not restricted by time or space.

---

* www.espresearch.com

This is an artist's tracing of a satellite photograph of the Semipalatinsk target site. Such tracings were made by the CIA to conceal the accuracy of detail of satellite photography at that time.

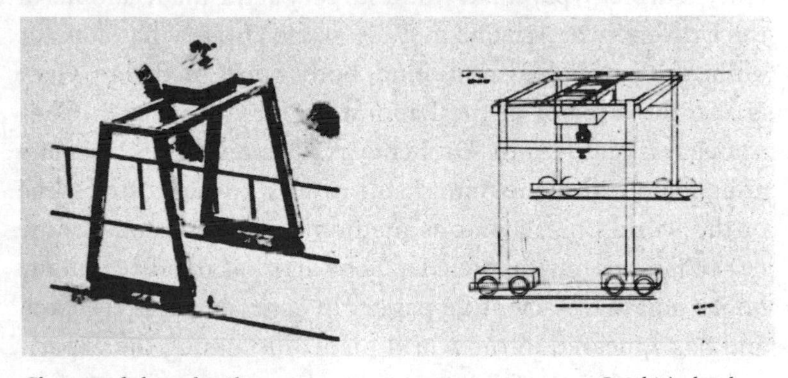

Close up of photo detail *Psychic's sketch*

On the right is a psychic's drawing of a gantry crane at the secret Soviet R&D site at Semipalatinsk, showing remarkable agreement with a CIA drawing based on satellite photography, shown for comparison on the left. Note, for example, that both cranes have eight wheels. (Remote Viewer: Pat Price. This trial was carried out with Russell Targ in 1974.)

J.B. Rhine, who founded the Rhine Research Center, was most notable for his series of experiments on Extra Sensory Perception using special *Zener cards* (each card bears one of five different symbols) with Hubert Pearce and J.G Pratt. Pratt tested Pearce using the Zener cards. Pratt shuffled and recorded the order of the cards in the parapsychology lab, which was situated 100 yards from where Pearce was sitting. The accuracy of Pearce's answers was incredibly high and this gave the scientists a yearning to experiment further with other psychic abilities. This is a test that you can replicate yourself. I would advise that you either make up your own Zener cards or substitute normal playing cards and you could try to identify the color of each card. After some practice, you could be able to identify the suit and perhaps even the value of the card itself. This is an excellent exercise to replicate the test conditions first used at the Rhine Center.

Gary E. Schwartz, Ph.D, is Professor of psychology, medicine, neurology, psychiatry, and surgery at the main campus of the University of Arizona in Tucson. He also teaches courses on health psychology and mind, body, spirit medicine. Gary is also the director of the Laboratory for Advances in Consciousness and Health. Dr. Schwartz has tested ESP and life after death with some remarkable results. He has tested some of the world's most famous mediums and, of course, some not so famous ones as well. Dr. Schwartz has published many books and many scientific papers in consciousness research and has appeared in the world media discussing the experiments. In 2007 Dr. Schwartz carried out a significant piece of research with regard to information received by mediums in a triple blind test. Julie Beischel, who founded the Windbridge Institute, now carries out the main research in afterlife communication.

The following is a little background information on the Mediumship testing. The information was taken directly from Dr. Schwartz' publication on the Internet.* This triple-blind study was designed to examine the anomalous reception of information about deceased individuals by research

* www.drgaryschwartz.com

mediums under experimental conditions that eliminate conventional explanations.

PARTICIPANTS: Eight University of Arizona students served as sitters: four had experienced the death of a parent; four, a peer. Eight mediums who had previously demonstrated an ability to report accurate information in a laboratory setting performed the readings.

METHODOLOGY: To optimize potential identifiable differences between readings, each deceased parent was paired with a same-gender deceased peer. Sitters were not present at the readings; an experimenter blind to information about the sitters and deceased served as a proxy sitter. The mediums, blind to the sitters' and deceased's identities, each read two absent sitters and their paired deceased; each pair of sitters was read by two mediums. Each blinded sitter then scored a pair of itemized transcripts (one was the reading intended for him/her; the other, the paired control reading) and chose the reading more applicable to him/her.

RESULTS: The findings included significantly higher ratings for intended versus control readings ($p = 0.007$, effect size = 0.5) and significant reading-choice results ($p = 0.01$).

CONCLUSIONS: The results suggest that certain mediums can anomalously receive accurate information about deceased individuals. The study design effectively eliminates conventional mechanisms as well as telepathy as explanations for the information reception, but the results cannot distinguish among alternative paranormal hypotheses, such as survival of consciousness (the continued existence, separate from the body, of an individual's consciousness or personality after physical death) and super-*psi* (or super-ESP; retrieval of information via a psychic channel or quantum field).

Basically, what this all means is that it is true and that no deception was used. Based on the collated information there would be no other means to identify the data other than to glean it from sources outside of consciousness. It means that there is life after death and that energy can be read either physically or through the spirit speaking to us through our spiritual faculties. This is the way that we mediums read for individuals—by a merging of minds, if you will.

Tailor Your Skills for the Martial Arts

I am not going to teach you how to develop all of the psychic gifts because it would fill a second volume and take a great deal of time to explain. Instead, I will concentrate on what I feel is necessary to *budo* and your martial training. Why am I the best person to teach you this? As well as being a martial arts practitioner for many years, I am also an internationally renowned psychic medium who uses these gifts on a daily basis. Let's begin to delve into the depths of the human psyche and develop our clairvoyant gifts through simple exercises.

Now For Psychic Development

This is probably one of the most important parts of the book, and the reason why you have it in your hands now. We will look at some general development exercises and then move on to exercises within the *dojo*. What I'm about to describe deals only with general development and those that know me and are reading this book will note how intensive my seminars and courses are and what I expect from students. It takes a lot of dedication and devotion to properly develop these gifts to full capacity.

The first thing that you need to know is that you must learn to protect yourself before opening yourself up to any external energies or influences. You must learn to ground yourself and then know that you are fully protected in all that you do. This will help you to develop your natural psychic ability. Now, don't worry—it's not because anything will "get into you," it's just that you can upset your energy field and cause emotional turmoil—which can be very upsetting on all levels.

Start with a Grounding Exercise

You have all taken part in the five-day meditation practice outlined on page 52, and should be well-versed in meditation by now. This exercise will be short and simple and I refer you to the grounding practice that we did before if you need to refresh your memory. We ground to ensure, through intent, that we are protected and free from the cords of negativity. This allows us to free the mind, body, and spirit to dance in the void, and sense and feel the subtle changes and nuances in our surrounding environment.

The importance of the breath is fundamental in all martial arts and this is also true of the development of your psyche. The breath holds many secrets. It is there at the birth of life and it's there at the last when we leave this plane of existence. The breath keeps us alive and part of this physical realm, it develops power internally and it helps to calm us when we need comfort. The breath is the key to enhancing our internal power or *ki*, and it is the key to entering the void to develop the powers of the soul.

Exercise: Back to Back

This is the first exercise that can be employed in the dojo and one of the exercises that I teach to my psychic development students. Work with a partner and ensure that this is someone that you do not know. Sit back to back with them and with intent ask for protection from your higher self. Also, see your auric field expanding with intent and overlap your partner's energy field. When you have done this and you are settled and happy with what you have done, answer the following questions:

1. What did your partner do three days ago? (Visualize this.)
2. What colors did they wear two days ago?
3. Visualize in your mind, then write down where your partner last went on vacation. What did they do there?
4. See an important event in their life and describe what happened—the description must be more specific than "a vacation," "a trip to the dentist's office" or "a party." This should be something like being given a special gift and what the gift was, a relationship with a favorite pet, etc.—what was it?
5. Visualize any medical conditions in their life—what are they?
6. What kind of car do they drive? (This question assumes that you don't already know the individual, and aren't already familiar with the cars parked outside. If so, try to visualize what car their partner or friend drives, instead.)
7. Give an important first or last name of a close family member, including how this individual is related.
8. Name a date that is important to the person.
9. What is a food they dislike?
10. What blockages do they have in their life that stops them from moving forward?

Practice this time and time again until you begin to record relatively high scores each time you do this, and do it with different individuals—especially those who you do not know. Then you can try the exercise with the reader blindfolded. Choose a random sitter or allow the reader to feel a personal possession belonging to the sitter.

Exercise: What's in the Envelope?

Take ten envelopes, five of which will have different, randomly-chosen photographs in them. Have a third party shuffle the envelopes and ensure they are securely sealed. Next, ask the person who is being tested to come forward. Allow some time for them to go within and then ask them to determine which envelopes contain no images, and to identify the images within the remaining envelopes. Each response should be discretely marked as a hit or a miss. An important thing is to understand is that you should not expect your reader to score 100% when they are only beginning to develop clairvoyant ability. Even if accurate, general information such as "blue color" is not precise enough to indicate maturing ESP and clairvoyant potential—what is the thing that is blue? However, if the reader is able to see the concealed images and identify several aspects of each—i.e. colors, shapes, and content—then this is an indicator that ESP and clairvoyant ability are present in the reader.

I was recently running a psychic development seminar in the US and one of the students blew my mind with his natural ability in remote perception. During the envelope exercise, he correctly identified three targets out of eighteen that were chosen at random by myself and known only to me. Instead of giving me a general idea of what could be perceived, he described exactly what was on each. I was deeply impressed by him and I hope he continues his path to development.

Remote Perception

Now we are going to move to the next stage as we look at clairvoyant ability and how it relates to identifying randomly chosen targets to remote perceive. This technique is also known as *remote viewing*, but I prefer the term *remote perception*. Parapsychologists Russell Targ and Harold Puthoff introduced the term in 1974, Dale Graaf emphasized it in his Stanford Research Institute early in the seventies, and I feel that it's appropriate that I should continue to use it now. What is this "remote viewing?" Quite simply, it is the ability to perceive information about a distant or unseen target using paranormal means or clairvoyance—extra-sensory perception.

Exercise: Where Am I?

Here is a basic exercise, which can easily be widened to include any number of students in the dojo. While it's not a true remote viewing exercise, it captures the essence. One member of the group should select random targets in your surrounding city or town; these targets should be kept secret from the other students. Dispatch students to each of the chosen locations. The remaining students should stay in the dojo and in a meditative state. Presently, each student should try to tune into the target areas in order to identify information pertaining to the given target locations where their fellow students are stationed. Each reader should either sketch the information that they're receiving, or describe it verbally.

This exercise will quickly pinpoint potential psychic ability of a very high standard if you are as strict as I am. You can have a great deal of fun with this, and you will immediately begin to identify your own inner gifts of clairvoyance. The key to success with this exercise is *complete* secrecy. Properly done, and with scientific controls in place, the results should convince even the hardened skeptics within your circle.

Exercise: I Hear a Name

This fun exercise will help you to identify the gift of clairaudience. Choose someone in the dojo that you do not know very well, sit back-to-back with them and with intent do the same exercise as detailed on page 52 in order to protect yourself. Bring in your protection and prepare yourself as aforementioned. This time you will tune into your partner's vibration and mentally ask your higher self to let you hear the names of individuals within the sitter's immediate and relative family. You will score one point for a direct hit on getting the name, and half a point for just getting the correct initial. Hearing clairaudient information is similar to the way you hear the words being imprinted on your mind as you are quietly reading. This is subjective clairaudience. Eventually you may be able to develop the ability to hear both first and last names of individuals, but this is very rare indeed. You may even develop the ability to clearly hear other dialogue from the spirit.

Exercise: What Am I Doing?

In the next exercise you will identify what your partner has done over the past week. As before, prepare yourself and tune into your partner's vibration. Then you will try to identify—using your psychic gifts—what your partner has been doing over a period of five days. You will start by tuning into each day intently and will ask your higher self to be shown what your partner did on that particular day. It could be something as simple as taking the dog for a walk. Perhaps you will see a clairvoyant image that is not random and can't be mistaken as luck or coincidence—such as changing a car tire on a particular day. You get the idea. For instance I would not score you very highly if you said, "He's been shopping"—that's far too general for me. But if you correctly said, "He's been shopping and bought a bottle of wine and a shirt," I would be inclined to agree that it was a direct hit and definitely clairvoyant. In fact, if you were that good, I would help you to develop professionally. Of course, you can also do this as a premonition exercise. To do so, you need to ask your higher self to show you what is going to happen to your partner in the next week. Foretelling your partner's future works the same way as seeing their past.

Exercise: Are They Attacking?

Here is an exercise that can be done in the dojo. Work in groups of three for this exercise. One of you must choose to be blindfolded, after which this individual should be given a chance to meditate and go within. The others will then stand in front of or behind the blindfolded individual, who will identify the point at which the "attackers' " intentions precede an attack. Now, be aware that the point is not to try to evade an attack—rather, the point is to identify the intention that precedes the physical manifestation and movement of the attack. The reason for this distinction is because otherwise, the sceptics will argue that correct answers were aided by audible cues. To make things even harder, have the blindfolded individual identify the "attacker" who gave the intention by name.

Exercise: Who Is Pointing?

This is a brilliant exercise to have fun with, and everyone in the dojo can take part in this. First of all, you will all have a short meditation as you sit in a circle. One individual will be chosen to sit blindfolded in the middle of the circle. At random times the *sensei* will choose an individual by nodding in their direction and that individual will silently point directly at the chosen student who is in the middle while simultaneously tuning in with their psychic intentions. Each direct hit scores one point. The winner is the one who has most points.

You can start a chart in the dojo and make it a friendly competition. To make it even more challenging, you can ask the person in the middle to tune in and give a psychic impression of the pointing individual's past or present conditions.

Psychic Technique

These exercises will help you establish a basic level of development that you can build upon. There are literally hundreds of exercises that I could cover, however, I'm limited in the amount of material that I can put into this book. As you try the exercises, you may or may not notice the changes in the dojo and in your training right away, but I guarantee you that you will begin to change subconsciously. You'll find that you can seamlessly move between techniques while maintaining intuitive connectivity. This connectivity keeps your mind, body, and spirit working as one. You will be able to identify the intent of the opponent, and your body will react without conscious thought. By this you begin to work in the *kukan* (empty space) of the void.

THE FIFTH RING

The Psyche — Evidence and Application

Eventually, there is a chance that in continuing your development, you will be able to break into the hidden realms of the spirit world. Note that Soke and masters in other *budo* disciplines recognize the reality of this world. In your meditation, a guide, angelic presence, or a deceased family member may visit you.

Messages from the Spiritual Realm

I always understood that I was a medium, natural by birth, but it was never something that was readily talked about in my life for fear of ridicule. Nevertheless, I developed and trained professionally later in my life. I would like to give you a few personal examples that show how messages passed in the dojo have a dramatic effect to the individual, both inside and out of the dojo. In these cases, I will use examples from my readings to students, including one that takes place outside of the dojo, with an individual who was thousands of miles away.

Ian's Story

Sometimes, the best readings—and the most touching in a person's life—do not occur not when the individual has arranged for an appointment to see me, but when the spiritual message comes unexpectedly. Ian's father popped in during training to offer comfort and love to his son.

> *Today started the same way as any other day. That is, up until the time that I got a call from Jock asking if I wanted to do some personal training. There was only Jock and Darren and I, and it was a good session, a completely different way of training—quite in-depth at times.*
>
> *However, what was to follow was mind blowing. We sat talking in the park when Jock asked me if I was getting a new van. Feeling a bit confused, I said that I had no plans to. When I asked him why, he looked over at my red van and replied that he could see a white one in its place. I pretty much brushed this comment off. Jock then asked about my parents and if my dad had passed away, which he had about four years ago. Jock paused for a few moments then said, "your father is here." I thought to myself, "right, okay." I am very open-minded to things, but there was part of me that said "no way." Anyway, we carried on and I was just blown away by how accurate Jock was with names, dates, times, issues and even some little traits that my dad had, not to mention his description of my dad's pet collie—right down to the name of the dog. It was a very emotional experience for me, and yet it helped to answer some questions that I never thought would be possible. There was no way that Jock could have known the stuff he told me, and I just want to*

thank him from the bottom of my heart for helping me, by using his special gift and for being an awesome teacher. It's been a privilege to be one of his students.

I would advise anyone who may be feeling a bit lost or in need of some answers to questions to heed Jock's advice. Even if you're a skeptical, you won't be disappointed. Oh, and one last thing—about a month after my reading I got a new red van... that actually used to be white.

— Ian K.

Andy's Story

Religion can also hold us back and block the spiritual communication that we receive. It is when these blockages and barriers are torn down that we can fully explore the innate potential in our lives and in our training. Fear is a major barrier, but it takes only small steps to conquer.

I have been a martial arts student of Jock's for almost a year. During that time he explained how he was a psychic and a medium. I have been with him when he received messages and passed them to others. Having lost my father at a young age, I wondered why I never got a message. My father was a religious man (being an elder in a church), and as a family we were heavily involved in the church, whether it was Boy's Brigade, Sunday School or Bible Class. I thought that perhaps my father would not approve of a medium reading because I believed that it was not a Christian practice. I thought about getting a reading for a long time. The pain of losing my father is still very present in my family and I thought that no one in the family would approve. Finally, I approached Jock and asked for a reading, explaining that my father had passed on. He agreed and told me he did not want to know any more background information. All Jock knew of me was that I had a wife and young son, I liked running and golf and worked as a taxi driver.

When the reading started, Jock was casually dressed, and sitting in his house. At the outset, I was a little anxious and unsure of what to expect. He immediately said there was a woman, Margaret or Maple or a funny Mabel-sounding name who passed with a mental condition or stroke, and she was cleaning at this moment. I told him her name was Mabel, my grandmother, who I was close to. Before her stroke, she was very proud of her house. Jock told me she is very headstrong and I thought, "yeah, that's Gran."

Jock told me she was bringing a man, Alexander. That was my father. Instantly Jock had problems breathing and asked if my father had a breathing problem. Before I could answer, Jock said my father died of an asthma attack, which was correct. Jock told me that father was very proud of me and loved me—something he did not say when he was alive and regretted it. The reading continued and Jock told me of exact dates, his death was in November and his wedding day was in September.

Jock reported that March was important for birthdays, which it was, as there are four family members who have birthdays in March. Apparently, April was also important, but I could not think of any reason for it to be. Later, Jock said to me, "your father said 'April' three times to me, so it is important." I suddenly realized that my wedding was in April. Jock explained that my father was sad that he could not be there, but knew that someone raised a toast in his name. As a matter of fact, my church minister, who knew my father very well, spoke about my father at the wedding, explaining how he was a family man and how he would have very proud of me and of my brothers. Jock told me my father also watched my first dance, which made me happy.

There were also times during the reading that made me laugh—something I did not expect. My father had been watching me one night when my son was feeling ill. I had been in a room with very low lighting, cuddling my son and singing to him. My father said my singing was terrible, out of tune. Jock also explained to me that my father loved "mince and tatties" [a popular Scottish dish made with minced beef and mashed potato] and would love to have some.

Jock continued to say that my mother still carried a lot of grief. My father asked me to tell my mother that he still loved her very much and asked me to send flowers. Lilies, irises and roses were important. A short time after his death my mother planted roses in the front garden, as my father loved roses. Jock also told me that my father and mother were into gardening, and my mother often thought of him when gardening. My father grew his own vegetables, and had a greenhouse. When Jock said that, all I could think of was my father's tomato plants that he grew every year. No sooner had I thought it, than Jock said my father was proud of his tomatoes.

I have to admit that I was a little skeptical of a reading because of my Christian upbringing. I did not know what I would be told, or if anything would be relevant to me. I have read that mediums can tell you information that can be applied to everyone. I was also aware how others can pick up on little signals of information when talking to you—something I learned to do when I was in sales. My family background information could be found out about me. However, as the reading continued, Jock talked about my family, dates, events, just a huge amount of information—some of which I was still remembering days later. I wanted to speak to my mother to verify what I had been told. I really found much of the information to be amazing, but four pieces of information really shocked me. There is no way that Jock could have known or found out about the following:

First, Jock said that my father wanted to give his regards to Pat. Pat was my father's friend and they used to swim together. For the past twenty years he's been taking me swimming every week. Jock then said something that surprised me, "he's still got it." Pat is 83 years old and a fantastic swimmer. At 83 he easily beats swimmers half, even a quarter of his age. I always say to Pat when he does a fast lap, "you've still got it."

Second, Jock told me that I saw a robin. Two days earlier, I did see a robin, staring at me with a big red breast. I made a mental note—the first robin of winter. Jock explained that it was a sign from my father. What shocked me later was a discussion I had with my mother. I did not tell her about the robin, but she told me that she always thought of my father as a robin. The first winter after my father died there was snow at the grave and there was a robin sitting on his head stone.

Third, Jock said my father liked music and said "old blue eyes." I remember that my father had a record player in the living room and some LPs. When I asked my mother, she told me that my father's favorite song was, "Don't it make my brown eyes blue."

Finally, Jock told me about my father wanting to give my mother flowers; lilies, irises and roses. I went to a flower shop and ordered flowers, but was disappointed to find out that the irises were out of season and would be a four day wait. Jock also told me about my father wanting mince and tatties. I was over at my mother's house after that: she was cooking mince and tatties for dinner. When we left my wife asked about the flowers in the garden, which looked like small leeks. My mother replied, "They are irises, which are unusual to see at this time of year." I had to smile.

I have carried a lot of emotional baggage with me for years, but since the reading I feel so much better. I know the expression, "a weight has been lifted off me" is corny, but I feel that it has. I like the thought that my father is close, watching over my family and me.

— Andrew Frazer

Christy's Best Friend Says, "Hi"

The letter below is in reference to a particular reading that was given to Christy, a Bujinkan member in Arizona. The reading was given over the computer while I was discussing seminars with her. Sarah—a person who was unknown to me and had passed fairly recently (within a few years) from breast cancer—was Christy's best friend and had popped in suddenly to say hello and let her know that she was okay. I was honored that Sarah chose to communicate through me that night.

The impromptu reading kind of caught me off guard. I wasn't expecting it, but Jock, you absolutely nailed it from the start. I guess Sarah really wanted to get my attention. And I can honestly tell you that prior to this, I have never had any sort of "official" readings done at all—I am somewhat paranoid when it comes to this area. The information you were relaying to me was so personal—no one else really knew. The fact that you actually pinpointed the personal item that I am getting in memory of her blew me away. The level of detail that you relayed literally made me cry. The stories you were aware of, the times that Sarah and I spent together... there is no way you could have known those things.

From start to finish Jock, I was almost speechless. I cannot express to you how much this reading meant to me, and it gives me a lot of peace, knowing that Sarah is okay.

Thank you, from the bottom of my heart. I look forward to seeing you soon!

— Christy, Arizona Bujinkan

Kris's Story

Here's another letter from an individual who received overwhelming evidence of the continued spiritual existence of family members who had passed on. I was able to be the medium through which their messages to her were transmitted, and as you'll read, I was also able to use my sixth sense in a practical way to resolve a frustrating situation.

Note: What I'm about to write is completely true. I have had an interest in psychic phenomenon for many years, so I have always been a bit leery of people who profess to be mediums or psychics—and I understand the techniques that charlatans use to trick people. During my time with Jock Brocas, he used none of these that I could identify. It is my opinion that he is one of the rare, true psychic mediums around in the world today and to my knowledge, the only professional medium that I know of in the Bujinkan.

My flight to the Highlands of Scotland was earlier than anticipated. I had arrived to assist and learn at a seminar that Jock was giving at the Bujinkan Taijutsu Dojo in Inverness. After finally arriving in the train terminal in Inverness in the early afternoon, this smiling giant of a man greeted me and introduced himself for the first time. It was Jock himself who'd come to fetch me.

I had been reticent about my trip, because my personal teacher who had been scheduled to teach had been forced to cancel after an injury just a few days before. Because of that I had waited too long to find accommodations for the weekend event. Jock was kind enough to drive me through half of Inverness searching out a room for me, and it gave us a wonderful opportunity to get to know each other. I had known beforehand that Jock was a psychic medium, but I had no intention of bringing the subject up, although we did discuss it briefly as we drove because we spoke about his book.

Anxious to find a place for me to stay, Jock suddenly remembered a small inn near his dojo, and we headed there. Fortunately, the inn had a vacancy—it was the sort of place you imagine you'd find in the highlands, but so rarely do.

After signing the guest register and accepting my key, I placed my meager belongings in the room, and invited Jock to share a cup of coffee with me in the sitting room, which looked out to a pasture filled with livestock grazing in the shadow of a Scottish hill.

It was early evening by now, but Jock and I had hit it off, and were enjoying each other's company when an odd look came over Jock as he turned his head to the right as though listening to something. I will not discuss the details Jock told me in detail, however I will provide a general overview.

He told me that there was a group of people coming through to him regarding me, concluding there were three. He then asked me specifically if I knew someone with an "M" in the name like Maria and if I knew an Anne or Annie. At the time I said no, my curiosity piqued. He told me to think again, because this spirit insisted it was there for me. I suggested perhaps my grandmother, Madeleine—but he said no. That wasn't it. I considered a bit, but was drawing a blank. Who else did I know with an "M" in the name that had passed on? He tried again, saying this person was very important to me. It didn't help. I was still very much at a loss until Jock himself identified her—it was my mother! My mistake was in thinking of her in terms of the nickname she had always used in life: Bibbi. But her given name was Anne-Marie! Once she was identified, Jock proceeded to ask me if I recognized bits of information, as he tried to interpret what she wished to tell me. In some cases I did, in some I didn't—but slowly her message came through to me.

During the conversation, my father, and my older sister also were identified correctly—although Jock could have no way of knowing that I had lost those three people in my life. It is of course possible he might have guessed that I'd lost my parents, but it is doubtful that he could have guessed that about my sister. He asked for confirmation on things which are, shall we say, less than typical—the sort of things that make people unique. Jock sat there for nearly an hour and a half as he interpreted the messages being given to him—a revelation to me, but nothing out of the ordinary for him. Toward the end however, both he and I were extremely tired. We would have our seminar early the next morning, so we ended our session there.

The next morning, we met in the hotel for breakfast and the conversation turned to my reading the previous evening. No sooner had we begun to talk than Jock was receiving messages again from the spirit world, and this time my father came through with one very important validation about a particular ring he had.

Now, I know that any general information could be gleaned and that most people wear rings. But what struck me was the evidential content when Jock said this was a ring that my father had and was not a wedding ring, he only wore it now and again and then in a further breath he said "It's some sort of fraternity ring." That was a direct hit.

There was one further incident over the course of the weekend, something that didn't even involve me, which was the best proof of legitimacy that I could have ever witnessed. While we were driving, a client called Jock because some very important papers had apparently disappeared including a passport—which he had already predicted. Jock, without missing a beat, proceeded to explain that the papers were nearby the person, located in a bag of some sort in the back of a locked cabinet in the bedroom, and finished the discussion. About an hour later, he was informed the papers were found, and were indeed where he said they'd be. I haven't met many people with the talent, or willingness to help people that Jock showed me that first weekend I met him. The things he told me were both accurate and helpful to me. I look forward to getting to know him better in the years to come.

— Kris Quinn, July 4, 2009, Harstad, Norway

Charlene's Brother Tends the Family

Spirits will not just come through to offer comfort and proof of their existence. Often they will see a need to teach lessons of forgiveness, and to rebuild the bridge to love and understanding. On this occasion, it was not my student who needed the message or the guidance. It was his immediate family and their relations where the need was most pressing. This can be a life-changing experience.

My husband Paul, who is a student of Jock's in the martial arts (Bujinkan), introduced me to Jock. Paul asked Jock to come around to check out the house and have a cup of tea. I was quite apprehensive about meeting him and wasn't sure what to expect. However, after just a few minutes Jock had brought my deceased brother through and confirmed that he had taken his own life back in 1996, an event that struck a devastating blow to the family. This tragedy left a lot of unanswered questions and doubts, and was always in the back of my mind. As you can imagine, this topic is a very emotional one for me, and I got a bit upset—this being the first time I had really confronted my feelings since my brother's passing.

The details from my brother were amazingly accurate: how I'd kissed a photo of my brother the day before when my husband's back was turned and had only thought about getting a tattoo of his name. This was something I'd never discussed with anyone—not even my husband!

A few months previous to this my family had a massive falling out, and I had suspended all contact with my younger brother—all this was mentioned through Jock with amazing accuracy: my deceased brother sought to resolve the situation.

Amazingly, after the reading, my family members contacted each other and we are all back on good terms and speaking to each other again. There were also messages for the rest of my family that Jock passed to me. Jock was 100% accurate in everything he told me and was very conscientious and caring throughout the reading, which helped put me at ease. Jock never asked for anything more than a cup of tea and a cookie in return for his help.

Jock has helped me and my family enormously in coming to terms with the passing of my brother, and also with other aspects of life in general. It is a comfort to us all to know that my brother is now happy and watching over us all. I have no hesitation in recommending Jock, as he is a genuine and gifted medium and we are honored to have him as a friend to our family.

Each one of these readings had dramatic effects on the individual. Did it help them in their training? Of course it did, although they may not have consciously noticed that part yet. Certainly anything that helps you to deal with life in a more positive manner—be it coming to terms with the loss of a loved one or resolving personal turmoil brought on by the external environmental factors—will undoubtedly help you in your training. It is true that your negative emotions and preoccupations will hinder your development in training, and being out of balance in life results in a loss of balance in the dojo.

Examples of Tactical Intuition

Musha shugyo is your warrior journey, your personal journey, your quest or your pilgrimage to find enlightenment. While studying, each person will change and grow along the journey—this is inevitable. Some masters have experienced their sixth sense in action and some students can also identify with this. I have already given you some historical examples of masters who have experienced this intuitive side of their psyche. Some other martial artists and masters in their own right have also directly experienced this in more modern times. Daniele Bolelli, author of *On the Warriors Path*, recounts an incident that occurred when he was leaving the dojo where he trained. A man he describes as being "not unlike a small mountain" approached him. This man had malice on his mind and asked Daniele which art martial art he studied, and if he thought it was good. His intuitive side was giving him signals from the pit of his stomach and he responded that it was only his first class and he did not yet know if it was any good. The outcome of the event was that Daniele listened to his inner feelings and diffused a potentially violent situation. Instead of a fight, he received directions and a free piece of gum! The "small mountain" chose another target from the dojo after Daniele left and proceeded to attack him after receiving the answer he expected.

Police Intuition

Dr. John Enger, a former police lieutenant commander and martial arts master recounted the following story for me:

> *How does a child explain their foreknowledge of things to come, or how they can sense bad or "evil" things in and around them, much less really understand what they are experiencing? That was my frustration! I always called it "knowing in my knower." I would try to tell my parents when I sensed things in my own life or others' lives. After some time attempting this I gave up trying to convince my parents, and kept everything to myself. I became a consummate introvert as I grew. I would "see" things in my mind's eye, dream things, and hear that small, still voice leading me regarding many different things. Crazy? Not hardly!*
>
> *So, what is one's "knower?" It's difficult to clearly define it. Nonetheless, it can be understood through the eyewitness reports of those who have accepted its existence and have let it become a part of their lives. These individuals rely on psychic knowledge to help protect and direct themselves and others who are willing to heed those who see and hear from within the soul. It's a gift that we all have, and one that's freely given by our Creator. You either receive a gift or you reject it. Some are acutely aware of their gift early in their lives, and I believe that this is yet another gift. Those who develop early are blessed with the opportunity help others develop what is already rightly theirs.*

I began to study the martial arts as a teenager, and I found the dojo to be a great place to hone my "intuitive knower" during sparring matches. I learned to "feel" what my opponent was about to do and had an adept way of avoiding being struck by kicks and punches most of the time. I began having fun just frustrating my opponents by having them chase me across the dojo. I never really thought much about striking or kicking back at the time—that was not my objective. It was a mental exercise for me and I was learning to develop a gift that I believe I had been given along with the skills that my sensei *was also imparting to me. Did it work all of the time? Absolutely not, but I can tell you that I was successful more often than not! I believe that anyone can learn to do the same: you can be taught to sense what the other person is about to do. They are literally transmitting messages to you without even knowing it. Tune in and you will hear it coming!*

Every law enforcement officer can tell you of stories of situations in their career where they narrowly avoided being injured or killed because of their level of training and skills they have received. There are also police officers who will emphatically tell you of situations where they acted upon "intuition" only, and because they did, it made a dramatic difference in the outcome of the call received or the investigation handled. Some officers clearly understand the gift they possess and yet others simply insist that they have a "gut feeling" or "hunch" at times but refuse to accept it as a part of their being or something that can be called upon any time they wish to use it. Let me share a brief story that kept me from being stabbed while responding to a "Burglary in Progress" call.

We had been having a number of break-ins to dollar bill changers in the district. The machines were being pried apart and large sums of cash being removed—not to mention the damage to the machines themselves. I mentioned to our detective division that I had real hunch (knew in my knower) that we should set up an alarm in a certain set of vending machines and a particular dollar bill changer in a specific building. They did so and nothing happened for over two weeks.

Then: I was driving into work one night to start my shift when I saw in my "mind's eye" a clear picture—a vision, if you will—of the area where the alarms had been set. The next thing I saw was a man running down a long corridor of that building carrying a very large mechanic's screwdriver in his hand while my partner was screaming over the radio that he was running toward the east exit. Then I saw myself standing in front of the suspect while he plunged the upraised screwdriver directly toward my face. I was immediately startled, panicked and caught off guard. The vision of this event ended there. I can tell you this: when I experience this type of thing, I take it to heart.

After this revelation, I got into work, poured myself a cup of coffee and pondered what I had experienced on the way in. At 11:00 PM I went to roll call, received my assignment, and was heading out the door to the squad car with my partner when we received—yes, you guessed it—a "Burglary in Progress" call from the very building with the set of machines on which the alarm was installed—the one that I saw in my "vision." My partner and I jumped into the squad car and he said, "I'll take the north set of doors and you cover the west set." "No," I responded, "if he runs I know he's going to the east exit." My partner trusted my instincts on this, and agreed. He pulled the squad car up a building away from where the call was dispatched. He headed toward the north set of doors and I ran around the building to the east exit. As I was running toward the east door I clearly remembered what I had seen earlier while driving into work—I knew what to expect! No sooner had I entered the door than I heard my partner scream over the radio that he was "running toward the east exit!" I drew my weapon. As the suspect rounded the corner he saw me and raised the screwdriver overhead. Although I would have been legally justified had I shot the man, I held my fire. After all, it would have been morally wrong—premeditation on my part—to shoot him because I knew what was going to take place in advance. Not being caught off guard, I was now in a position to disarm the suspect, which I did by sweeping his feet out from under him. He hit the ground quite hard—so hard, in fact, that he dropped the screwdriver and was disoriented.

A warning was given to me! I believe that, had I not taken seriously what I saw on the way in to work that night, I would have been startled by how quickly the burglar rounded that corner, caught off-guard, and injured or killed. Perhaps the vision prevented the suspect from being shot and killed as well. What I can emphatically say is that I had a premonition about where the burglar was going to strike again in the weeks leading up to this particular event, after which I foresaw the event in a vision that warned me of impending danger. As a result, no one was seriously injured or killed!

To all who weren't aware of the existence of this gift, you are now. It's resident within you. Fine-tune it for the good of mankind. It's free—a gift from your Creator!

A Walk up Alvarado

Deception and confusion can make a real difference in a confrontation. Martial arts are not just about technique and violence. In my mind, the highest level of martial artistry is the ability to defuse and defeat without having to move a muscle in retaliation. Using your mind and spirit is the expression of true *budo* and is parallel to using the natural intuition we all have, but some recognize it as something different—quite a paradox!

I remember walking up 6th Street toward Alvarado one night when I was 18 or 19 years old. I was across the street from the northeast corner of McArthur Park in Los Angeles. This area was a hotbed for all kinds of questionable activity at the time. Newly arrived immigrants from El Salvador, Guatemala and Nicaragua were showing up in the area daily. The guys on the other end of the park carried around stacks of Social Security cards, and as long as you looked like you might need one they'd flag you down like a drug dealer hoping to make a sale. They'd refer their clientele to other document mills along Alvarado St. where you could get a fake driver's license.

I was headed to get a burrito at this place that was open 24–7. I can't remember the name of the place, but it didn't have a front door and it only had bars for windows. You paid your money to someone on the other side of a thick shield of Plexiglas. Adding to the general feeling of malice that this part of town evoked, there had recently been a violent incident at this location, and blood had been spattered clear across the window. When I got there that night I was a bit anxious at this recollection, but I ordered a couple of burritos and got out of there.

At the time I couldn't get enough of this place, and this part of town. Everybody I met along the route I traveled to get my burrito "fix" was a character. The whores, the dealers, the addicts, hustlers, the freed felons, the bums and the mentally ill were all so much more interesting than the people where I grew up. Even the average corn-on-a-stick vendor had more character in his face than in most others I'd seen elsewhere.

As you can see, going to get a burrito was more of an adventure to me than an ordeal. I had no car so I had to walk, but I'd done this many times. On this particular afternoon I was just walking down the street with my food while the roar of the rush hour traffic buzzed beside me. I really couldn't hear much. I did have my "observer" on, though. I called the part of me that feels everything around me my observer. My observer was set at about a 5 foot radius, completely surrounding me.

I developed my observer through the limited taijutsu *training that I'd received at the time. The observer was always on from the moment my feet hit the pavement. This part of my training proved to be very useful, as I'll explain.*

As I was walking, for some reason I jumped back into Ichimonji no Kamae *(a common* taijutsu *posture). At that very moment, a guy sped by on his ten-speed—right through the space I would have occupied had I not acted so quickly. "You could've knocked me right off this bike!" he shouted behind as he passed by. Whoa. I wasn't scared, I wasn't angry, I wasn't really feeling anything but perplexed, perhaps.*

I'm forty-three years old now. I've long since moved away from that wretched neighborhood. For all of the stress that living there inflicted upon me, the environment served to sharpen my awareness like nothing else could. I was aware of every shadow approaching, and my observer became skilled in quickly sizing people up and performing threat assessments in terms of three dimensional space and distance. I don't call this intuition. I say it wasn't intuition because there was no thought involved. There was no lead-up cognition. There was just an instantaneous and innate response to something that was a threat.

Looking back, I wonder if I'd have the same response now. That was twenty-five years ago. I have to admit I don't put up my observer much anymore. At the time of this incidence I was young man without much money and no way to pay for the martial arts training that I wanted. Times changed, money came around, and I started training again.

In the summer of 2009 I had the opportunity of a lifetime. I was going to Noda City, Japan to take a very important test from one of the greatest living martial arts masters: Soke Masaaki Hatsumi. His diminutive dojo is like a little UN of ninja from around the world. At any given time you'll find gaijin *from just about anywhere. In order to be promoted in rank after 4th degree black belt, it is required that one sit for a test either administered by Soke Hatsumi or by one of his master teachers while Soke watches.*

The test involves turning your back to the teacher and facing more than 100 students from around the world while he or one of his students stands behind you and attempts to hit you over the head with a bamboo sword. The tension is palpable in such a moment and place. So much depends on what you are about to do or not do. You cannot think your way out of it. It's over in a moment and you either pass or you fail.

On a particularly hot August Sunday afternoon I sat for the first time for this test. My teacher stood behind me and waited with the sword held above his head, ready to cut down. Seconds passed, then suddenly an urge. I rolled and turned to look, but he had not cut yet. Again, we repeated the process. Again, I rolled and looked back and yet still he had not cut. I felt something was wrong. I sensed that a cut was coming and wondered how this could be. Finally, on the third cut I rolled and turned and he had cut down. I was elated but then I heard Soke say, "No!" I was really confused at this point. I rolled, my teacher had cut, and I wasn't hit. Certainly, there must be some mistake. I was sure that I had passed. Later, I was given another chance with one of Soke Hatsumi's top student teachers. He cut down and I moved out of the way and avoided being hit. To my surprise Soke again said, "No."

It was only later after discussing this with my teacher that I thought that I understood why I had not passed. My teacher told me that each time I had rolled it was when he had the intension of cutting me. The intention and cutting down were to separate things. I had rolled away on the intention and not the immediate threat. It was Friday of that week, and the day before going home when I finally passed the test. I used the observer once again. I created my radius and waited. I felt the intention to cut after a few seconds, but this time I didn't budge. I waited, as I was sure the cut would soon follow. The sword cut through the field surrounding me, and without conscious thought I rolled—and came up to applause. My case looked pretty hopeless, but the nice thing about people in the Bujinkan is that they are rooting for you. All their best wishes come to you.

This test is different for everybody, and the way that it went down for me is my own experience alone. Some people have no clue what is going to happen to them and they move and avoid the cut for their own unknown reasons. Others get cracked on the head and go home. Although I had moved out of the way of the original cuts, I moved for the wrong reasons. I was moving based on sensing an intention. As long as the intention and the cut happen simultaneously that would work. The essential problem with sensing an intention and responding to it rather than responding to an actual threat is clear to me now. A person may have the intent to kill you now, but may choose to do so at a time of his choosing. That may be in five minutes, next week or next month. To get a reaction out of you may set you up for something else. This was a great life lesson for me. It is what Soke Hatsumi taught me from this process. Had I passed the first day, I would have been overjoyed, but I would not have learned this lesson. I am happy that Soke Hatsumi was so discriminating in his supervision of my test, and allowed me work this out.

> *I feel like I've come full circle since the days of walking up Alvarado Street to get a burrito. My observer was not detecting any intention to harm me that day when I jumped back to safety. I was just aware of my surroundings in a heightened way. With only a few years of training then compared to many more since, it seems strange that I needed to be reminded of that time when the streets I walked were not safe and the warrior within me was aroused on my way to get a bite to eat.*
>
> *— Dr. James Clum, Shidoshi*

Now what James calls his "observer" is, in fact, intuition; for intuition does not dance around or play with conscious thought. This type of energy is not a thought process—it is way beyond the scope of conscious thought, and is in fact a part of the super-consciousness. Intuitive energy moves so fast that it is impossible to catch it consciously. Your intent can switch it on or off, but for the most part—when you have developed your sixth sense—intuition will work twenty-four hours a day, seven days a week.

THE SIXTH RING

Spiritual Warriorship

What does it mean to be a warrior in these modern times? I often explain to my students that if you have the knowledge and skill to kill, and are ever faced with that terrible decision to strike out (or not), deciding to show mercy to your opponent is certainly tantamount to being a true warrior. Moreheiba Ueshiba asserts that "solving problems before they form is the way of the warrior." To look beyond the mediocrity of the material world and see the beauty of what is there is true warriorship. Seeing the miracle of life around you and knowing the divine nature of it is true warriorship. Showing kindness, respect, humility and being mindful is also being a true warrior. Learning to forgive is the pinnacle of becoming a true warrior.

Being a warrior is not about how many battles you have won or how much knowledge you have of combat. As Sun Tzu wrote "Those who win by fighting are not truly skilled. Truly skilled are those who win without fighting." Becoming a skilled fighter and winning every conflict will mean nothing if you allow life to defeat you at every point. Living your life in grace and happiness does not need to be a battle either. Studying *budo* and the martial way allows us to leave this type of obsession behind, so we can live life the way it was meant to be.

What follows are my warrior beliefs or rules.

A Warrior Is Mindful

Unfortunately, most of humanity does not understand what it means to be mindful. Once this concept is understood and applied, it can change your life dramatically. Being mindful also helps us with the recognition of our internal spirit and reminds us who we are; in this way we can develop our spiritual gifts to the maximum. Mindfulness is a calm awareness of the body and of consciousness, emotions and feelings. This term is derived from ancient Sanskrit and is prevalent in Buddhist practices.

Thich Nhat Hanh writes:

> *"Mindfulness is the miracle by which we master and restore ourselves. Consider, for example: a magician who cuts his body into many parts and places each in a different region—hands in the south, arms in the east, legs in the north, and then by some miraculous power lets forth a cry which reassembles whole every part of his body. Mindfulness is like that—it is the miracle which can call back in a flash our dispersed mind and restore it to wholeness so that we can live each minute of life."**

By becoming a mindful warrior you let go of material gain, politics, forced beliefs, and mediocrity. You recognize that you are the captain of your own ship and have the internal power within you. However, being mindful is more—it is also about

---

* From *The Miracle of Mindfulness* by Thich Nhat Hanh. Beacon Press, 1975.

gratitude. For instance, think about the simple act of doing something in the dojo or in your daily life. Are you really in that moment; are you mindful of what you are doing, of your body, what you are saying, and the state of your mind? Can you give thanks to God for bringing you to this place? Have you given a thought for those that have gone before you in order that you can be brought this amazing gift of learning and of being at one with yourself? Think about this too; most people go about their daily lives just reacting to outside stimulus in a conscious manner. If an individual goes for a walk in the country, does he see the miracle of life before him? Oftentimes, no! He walks to get to his goal—the destination. This is a reflection of his life. His only goal is to successfully get to the end, and on that path he may miss the miracle of life that is his own creation. The mindful warrior will walk that same path but will see the miracle of life around him in all directions. He will see the sky, he will feel the earth beneath his feet and know that at that moment he is walking on a miracle. He will see the beauty in the trees and the foliage around him and will know the miracle of life. With every breath he takes, he will feel and sense the miracle of life around him and it will pervade his mind, body and soul. At that moment, the mindful warrior will realize that he is a part of God; he is that spark of divinity that is creationism itself, and he will give thanks for the miracle surrounding him. In this way the warrior is mindful.

I learned this lesson in a most profound manner. One day while I was in town waiting to meet someone, I watched the people around me and recognized that many had no inner awareness. Instead of being happy, their moods were governed by outside forces. All around me concerns about business and time governed everyone. No one seemed to have time for anyone else and people became agitated at the smallest things—creating an atmosphere of negativity around them. I asked

God to show me the beauty in the world even in this industrial jungle. Just then, a beautiful butterfly landed on the path in front of my foot and I bent down to get a closer look—it flew onto my body. In that instant I knew God had answered my prayer, and through the clouds broke a ray of sunshine. I realized then: martial arts are more about awakening to the self and to the miracle around, than they are about combat. To see the beauty in something that seems negative is the same as re-directing the energy of an angry opponent. Sometimes a smile, a nice thought or even pointing to something quite beautiful can change the direction of the possible altercation. My good friend Papasan (Ed Martin, Shihan) once recounted this story to me that exquisitely illustrates this point:

This friend of mine, Larry, was sitting on the front porch of his girlfriend's house in a very "rough" part of Albuquerque. Across the street from him a very large Mexican man was on his front porch along with a bunch of his buddies. It was later confirmed that this was part of a street gang—not the bunch you want to tangle with! There is a lot of tension between the "Anglos" and "Mexes" in Albuquerque—such stupid attitudes exist in many places.

*Larry was just looking off into the distance, when the man yelled across the street to him: "What the f*** are you looking at?" Larry just ignored him in the hope that the man would lose interest. However, the man jumped off his porch and started across the street toward Larry, again yelling, "What the f*** are you looking at?" Larry told me that what went through his mind was, "When that guy gets here he'll get the surprise of his life, although I know he's thinking, 'I'm going to kick that white guy's a**.' " By this* *time the man had crossed the street and got right in Larry's face, yelling at him again, "What the f*** are you looking at?" Larry told me, "I don't know where it came from but I said, "Aren't the mountains beautiful?" Caught off guard, the man turned around and looked at the mountains. He was so impressed with the view that he forgot all about the altercation that he'd come across the street to start. He went back to his house and took all of his buddies into his back yard so they could look at the mountains too.*

The next day he gave Larry a big smile and a "thumbs up." For the next two weeks, every time he saw Larry he would ask, "Hey man, are you okay? Can I do anything for you? Do you need anything for your car?" Now that is ninjutsu! That is the highest form of "martial art"—taking someone who is determined to be your enemy and making them think that they are your friend.

A Warrior Is Relaxed and Self-confident

A warrior is always relaxed and has inner confidence. When a warrior is relaxed, he is in control and is mindful of every action. His six senses are dancing around together like the vibrating atoms that comprise all of creation. In this way his senses are open to outside vibrations and, in an instant, the warrior can react intuitively rather than sluggishly, under the heavy burden of conscious thought. An opponent who wishes to attack you will never attack in a relaxed state of mind, for the very nature of attack is aggression. He is poised like a coiled spring waiting to go off and his intention is a build up of nervous energy in his spirit. The relaxed warrior will, of course, sense this and will move according to energy and not conscious thought. The way that the mindful warrior remains relaxed and radiates self-confidence will make the opponent angrier and more negative as he fails to achieve his goal. Thus, the mindful warrior is able to protect and move accordingly, forcing the opponent to defeat himself. In this way, we become peaceful warriors and not soldiers of combat.

A Warrior Does Not Worry

A warrior should not worry, for he knows that a force higher than himself is guiding him. We generally tend to worry about things that have no real meaning in life. Most times we dwell on concerns that we can't change at that particular moment. We need to recognize that we generate our own anxiety through internal emotional turmoil. In so doing we create the negative energy that builds up in our aura and makes us take wrong paths and make poor choices. Worry is an emotion that can hold you a prisoner of the self; it can cause physical manifestation of disease and will lower your immune system. The warrior never worries, for he knows that he will be guided along the path of life. He knows that the universe will provide all he needs, and his intuitive voice is there to communicate with the voice of guidance.

A Warrior Is Self-disciplined

A warrior is self-disciplined and will not put things off to tomorrow that can be done today, for he knows that tomorrow will never come. The warrior is able to keep sacred the time he reserves for meditation and will work to develop his inner wisdom and intuition. A mindful warrior knows that he is in control of all his faculties and is able to face fear with a clear mind and utilize the emotion as a weapon. A warrior keeps sacred his time to train and develop mind and body in the dojo, and does not allow the small things to keep him from this important task.

A Warrior Is Grateful

A warrior gives thanks for everything; he shows gratitude for even the small things. In showing this gratitude, the warrior grows in grace and in peace. Even the smallest pebble in the water can create a ripple effect throughout the whole pond. So with the smallest grateful thought we create positive ripples in our own pond that attract the same.

A Warrior Believes

A warrior does not follow any man-made belief system, but instead follows his heart and his own spirit. He uses his spiritual gifts to make wise life choices and to ensure that he is the epitome of peacefulness, toleration, and compassionateness.

A Warrior Co-creates

A warrior realizes that he is co-creator of his own life and destiny. He knows he has the ability to be the creative force that is life itself. He is able to harness the wisdom of the divine and his spiritual gifts to create the world he *wants* to live in instead of remaining shackled to a world he *has* to live in. He is able to bring peace to a discontented heart.

A Warrior Is Devoid of Ego and Desire

The warrior realizes that his ego is the nemesis of his martial way; he knows that he must be devoid of ego if he is to rise above the mindless control that is all around him in the world. The ego will, if allowed, force martial skill to be controlled by emotion and not heart. Only when devoid of the ego does the warrior allow himself to be guided by his heart and therefore open himself to the wisdom of *budo* and the righteous virtues it upholds.

A Warrior Gives Service

The mindful warrior gives service to humanity and uses his skills not for combat but to protect the good and righteous virtues of humanity. He must only draw the sword when protecting his fellow man, family or for the highest good. He never reacts in anger and will help those in need, knowing that every good pebble cast in the water creates a positive ripple with which to remove evil and negativity from the world. His skills are a gift of the divine and his award is the service to humanity and not himself. In this way the warrior is selfless and spiritually evolved.

A Warrior Is Humble

A warrior is humble and knows how to recognize his own faults and misgivings, he understands that in the quest for enlightenment, he will have to face inner turmoil in order to be able to work on those issues by being aware of them and of himself. The warrior knows that in his humility he is able to deal with life in a more productive way. He seeks divinity rather than riches and delights in the good fortune of others.

A Warrior Forgives and Is Compassionate

The most important aspect of warriorship is to learn to forgive. Lack of forgiveness harbors negative emotion in the soul, and negativity leads to fear—and fear feeds on itself. The lack of a forgiving spirit can lead to all sorts of problems in one's life: physical, emotional and mental. If the characters of God, Jesus, Buddha and Krishna can all be described as forgiving, even to those who falter, then as sparks of divinity we should be able to be the same way. In this way we practice the mindfulness of peace of heart. Perhaps this is also an element of *kyojitsu* (truth and falsehood). You cannot forgive anyone else unless you forgive yourself, and you restrict your natural spiritual growth if you are unable to show compassion and forgive. All you have to do is ask for forgiveness with real intent and pure heart and it is granted.

The warrior is compassionate and shows this compassion to all of God's creation, he sees the beauty behind the negativity and understands the desires that drive man. He neither judges nor ridicules and is accepting of everything and everyone who shares this earthly home.

The various virtues described above are ones that I uphold and feel that every student should recognize, for it's by living these virtues that we come to realize our true nature and understand who we really are. In this way we get to become one with ourselves and the totality of nature. Our gifts, therefore, are not those of duality, but are exactly the opposite. The sixth sense becomes our primary sense and the other five only serve to highlight the power of the intuitive nature that we actually possess.

You Have the Power to Change

By living your life in the virtuous ways of the warrior and developing your psychic gifts that are, after all, a part of your natural spirit, you are able to live a life that is harmonious, abundant and blessed. Everyone has their own problems that they are dealing with every day, but even small problems can be exacerbated and become larger than you can control. To conquer these problems, you need to have the desire and the will to change. A good master can only offer the student the keys to the door: you must be willing to walk up and open the door. You must also realize these lessons from the dojo can be applied to your life, and you do not have to be a *budo* practitioner to understand them.

Letting Go of the Ego

Okay, I have discussed the ego a number of times in the book and I would like to point out that the word conveniently forms a relevant acronym: "Edging God Out" which, in effect, is you too. The ego seeks to destroy the belief in yourself as it taunts you like a court jester. It will make you feel uneasy, unworthy and will instill in you that feeling of doubt in everything you do. Because of this you become a prisoner of the self and fail to meet your potential to co-create happiness, success and wealth in your life. It will tell you that you never have what it takes and—as mentioned before—your ego will make you feel that you are going nowhere with your *budo* training. Your ego does not want you to forge your mind, body and soul by studying the martial way because then you won't need it. It will go away crying, kicking and screaming for attention like a child. This suggests, perhaps, a method of visualization and intent that you can use in order to quiet your ego.

You must realize that the ego is a part of you and you should love it just as much as you love yourself. In order to control your ego you must show it your love, and when you get these kinds of thoughts during your training you will be able to recognize them and quiet them down by realizing that they are only discursive thoughts. For example, I once watched one of my students trying to replicate exactly what I was trying to teach in a class. Each time he would screw up his face as if he was thinking, "*I can't get it, I will never move that way.*" This, of course, was his own discursive thought process. How can we get rid of it?

Mindfulness is one way in which we can control our ego. To paraphrase words of the Buddha, "When you hold a cup of tea, then hold it and stay with it in the moment you are drinking." Buddha provided guidance for establishing mindfulness. Mindfulness—as we have discussed previously—is about bringing one's awareness to focus on the present moment and state of mind. Mindfulness is a way of controlling discursive thoughts and bringing your awareness to the oneness within. Your mind is at war with mind chatter and the ego. By noticing that the mind is continually creating an internal dialogue of discursive thoughts, one has the ability to carefully observe those thoughts, seeing them for what they are without judgment. One thing you must realize is that thoughts are just that—thoughts. You are free to recognize and release a thought because it becomes nothing more than that, without will, feeling, belief or emotion. So let it go and realize that it is not you.

You are then free to become an observer rather than getting caught in your negative mindset. In this way you can rise above your false beliefs and know that you can achieve anything you put your mind to. You can see that there are no mistakes that occur within the dojo and in your training—there are only opportunities for growth and expansion of the mind, body and soul.

"In our consciousness, there are many negative seeds and also many positive seeds. The practice is to avoid watering the negative seeds, and to identify and water the positive seeds every day."* Thinking is just a discursive habit—the real gift is discernment of mind.

Nourish Your Seeds

You can envision seeds as the beginning of your journey toward understanding the *Kihon Happo*, which is the fundamental basis of *budo*. Eventually, with the right conditions, your seeds will begin to develop their first roots, which will travel down to anchor themselves in the earth. With the right

---

* From *Anger* by Thich Nhat Hanh. Riverhead Trade, 2002.

nutrients and natural, non-obstructive energy, you will see the seeds begin to grow and reach beyond their initial limitations as they yearn for the natural energy and light of the sun. Notice, on the seeds' journey, how they need the right nutrients and commitment to be nurtured—not only from mother earth, but also from those who tend the garden. With the proper conditions, they develop strong roots that continually grow and develop greater strength. This, to my mind, is part of the essence of the *budo*.

However, we can inadvertently provide our seeds with the wrong nutrients and the wrong conditions, and while you feel like you are making progress in life, you are in fact holding yourself back. If you try to nourish your seeds of *budo* with negativity, this negativity can manifest in many forms. I know this from personal experience. If you have been feeding your seeds with negativity, you need to make the choice not only to grow, but also to seek happiness through enlightenment. Our primordial instinct to destroy and hunt is not the reality of human essence; it is merely an illusion. Negative self-talk can be as sharp as a blade, and can cut just as cleanly—right through your being. Many feed their seeds with negative thoughts and actions, and remain oblivious to their own natures.

The essence of *budo* is seeing the very nature of reality in the sixth dimension and not merely by what you touch. The void is within you, it is the divine you. Though your ego places you before others around you, I ask you to perceive with eyes of the mystic rather than of the merchant, who is only interested in material goals. The greatest sin that one can commit on earth is the denial of the eternal divine spirit.

If you allow them to, seeds of jealousy, anger and hatred will grow within, and the more you become enticed by the false beliefs of others who have already fed their own seeds of negativity, the more likely you are to produce a veritable forest of negativity. This negativity is a destroyer of the self, and will at some point manifest itself in the dojo and in your life, eventually destroying you from the inside out. It is important to understand awareness and to know that when you are aware of your negative thoughts, it is better to transform them than it is to try to deny them or destroy them.

Why do you constantly strive to win when your winning will only bring suffering to the other person? Why judge when you have no right to judge anyone other than yourself? In judging others, you are denying the weakness in yourself while placing yourself above all others. In so doing, you resemble a weed in the garden. Despite possessing a form of beauty, the judgemental "weed" is destructive in nature because of greed and malignancy. The stronger your inner seeds become through proper feeding with the right thoughts, actions and conditions, the less likely you are to be the target of those with negative seeds. You'll find that you receive and give back only positivity, which can help to transform the negativity around you.

Be mindful of your thoughts and your actions, and only feed your seeds with love, acceptance, happiness and understanding. Understand that we are all on a journey and that winning or proving yourself above others is the fertilizer that feeds the seeds of negativity within your spirit. *Budo* is perhaps the essence of life and an expression of the divinity within you, so feed your *budo* with the purest of thoughts and actions so that you may understand your own interconnectedness with the rest of creation.

Budo Is Happiness

When you enter the dojo to train and learn the various life skills of *budo,* it is one place where religion and false belief have no place. It is the only place where you can immediately leave everything that is associated with the "rat race" behind you and be at one with your mind, body, and soul. I'm not saying this is the *only* way; this is *one* of the ways—for you can experience much in other disciplines. But for those who study *budo*, it is one time when you can truly receive and feel real happiness. You should experience an "a-ha! moment" when you come to the realization that you don't really need to search for happiness—the happiness is within you and only takes the mingling of the mind and body in the dojo to reach that state of nirvana.

Ask yourself how you really feel inside when you have achieved something in the dojo that you thought you could not do, or perhaps finally carried out that form or *kata* in the correct manner and with the correct feeling.

You Get What You Give

One of the hallmarks of the martial arts is that it demands a great deal of effort be put into the physical aspects of the training. Your training will give you excellent results such as getting fitter, stronger, and faster—and in this way you forge the body into a working piece of art. The thing you must realize is that you also have to put the same dedication and discipline into developing the spirit for your highest possible good within your life. The sixth sense will then manifest realistically, and will no longer seem to be the feeble idea of new-agers and psychics. Even if you remain skeptical, you will find that you do have a higher awareness, and whether you call it your "observer," your "knower," or your gut, you will have to face the fact that it is your natural intuitive side that you have developed for the betterment of yourself and of humanity.

Give this some serious thought: if you put too much food into your body, you will undoubtedly become fat, lethargic and unfit, and will "reap what you sow" (another spiritual law).

By meditating and becoming one with yourself and with nature, you will develop your psychic ability to its fullest potential—your body will move without conscious thought. What's more: you will be able to make wiser life choices and take the right paths to your benefit and that of those around you.

Your Psychic Choice

Okay, so you've forged your indomitable spirit in the dojo and you have meditated and developed your intuitive senses to the extent that your taijutsu is not one of conscious thought and selective movement. You are relatively happy and you see how all this training can come to one important crescendo in the dojo, "but what about life?" I hear you ask. Well, through your training in *budo* or your chosen martial style, you will find that everything in the dojo is a reflection of your life, as I have previously mentioned. But all that training and intuitive sense development has much more to give you in your everyday life.

Wiser Choices Are Informed by Intuition

Imagine that you have decided that you are going to buy a new car, but instead of going to a show room you realize that you could get a great bargain by buying a used one from a private dealer. Now, you have scanned all the newspapers and browsed all the websites that are selling the kind of car that you seek. After hours or perhaps days of searching you find one that you really love. You make that phone call or send that email that tells the seller that you're really interested in what they have to offer. You get a response and you make arrangements to meet and view the car. You meet the person and everything feels as it should. He seems like a nice person and appears to be honest. However, the moment you shake his hand you don't feel so good, and you hear a voice in your head saying, "dealer." Following this, you receive a clairvoyant image of a car lot. What do you do? Do you listen to your psychic vibes or do you deny them and possibly purchase a lemon? You see, the universe has responded by sending you subtle signs. You have that free will to choose whether to heed the warning or not.

Sensing Danger

Obviously, you have the free will to listen—or not. In a moment you will read about an experienced *budo* practitioner and former student of many Japanese masters who failed to heed his intuitive warnings. Your psychic vibes are there to protect you and keep you, your family, and on a larger scale, humanity safe from harm. The challenge that we face is learning how to recognize these subtle cues and signs that surround us on a daily basis. How do we know that we have received a warning? In my previous work, *Powers of the Sixth Sense,** I go into great detail about our ability to sense danger. Here, I will add the following: in the dojo we train to heighten our awareness so that we are able to protect ourselves from attack. This is the job of intuition, my friends—prevention really is better than the cure. When we ignore our intuitive senses, the consequences can be disastrous, as you will now read.

One of my students (Chris) told me of an incident that happened in Fort William in Scotland. Chris had been a student of *budo* for many years and had spent time in Japan studying many disciplines, including the Bujinkan, which is what he chose. Chris was walking back from the supermarket with a box of groceries when a group of young guys began to gather in his path. His intuition was telling him to cross the road to avoid them, which he consciously ignored. After all, crossing

---

* Brocas, J. *Power of the Sixth Sense: How to Keep Safe in a Hostile World.* Great Britain: O Books, 2008.

would involve a detour, and he felt he was probably just being paranoid (the area was a small, semi-rural town and not a stereotypical city center). As he passed the group they surrounded him and one tried to grab the box of groceries, and then grabbed Chris. As he foolishly bent down to put the box on the ground, the little thug maneuvered Chris into a headlock and attempted to knee him in the face, as the degenerate bystanders shouted encouragement. Chris defended against this, and then escaped from the headlock. Unfortunately, he came up into an *ichimonji*-type guard position, which prompted the youths to throw some poorly aimed punches. Fortunately, in the end, Chris was able to escape. He called the police and went hunting for the perpetrators with them. They found one of the group who was so shocked that he informed on the rest of them!

Chris received a very clear sign from his intuition that he chose to ignore. He attributes his intuitive development to years of *budo* training and meditation. Unfortunately, his macho ego convinced him to do otherwise. You have the free will to heed either your ego or your intuition—I know which I would choose.

Exercise: Danger Is Near

Let's put some of this knowledge into practice by taking part in a danger exercise. This is not a game, but it can be a gratifying way to learn very valuable lessons that may save your life. The primary challenge you will face is that the individuals who are chosen to be the ones broadcasting a negative intention need to know how to effectively build and send that intention. This exercise won't be successful otherwise. Therefore, it takes a bit of mental preparation to make this work.

The exercise organizer should choose a secure area, but one that is also evocative of danger: lots of cover, ambush potential, and dim lighting all help to set the scene. Potential locations include parks, dark car lots, and city environs. This must all be done in total secrecy to ensure that the exercise is run under scientific conditions, therefore lending support and validating evidence for your intuition. It is also a good idea for the organizer to let the police know that this exercise is going ahead to avoid the possibility of false alarms or law enforcement misunderstandings.

After you've settled on the locale, choose who will be going through the exercise and who will be the attacking force. The students chosen to transmit the negative intention need to be segregated from the others taking part in the exercise. They will have to take some time to get into the mindset of a murderer, rapist, or terrorist. After they are adequately prepared, this "hunter force" should be dispatched to the chosen ambush points. The hunter force must continually reinforce their mental negativity so that they're strongly broadcasting their intention to attack a weak and helpless individual. The students who are now segregated from the hunter force should be told that they are going to conduct an exercise that involves moving in the dark. As far as they will be aware, this will be a *taijutsu* exercise—not a sensing one—so they will be unprepared.

Under very tight conditions, instruct each student to walk along a predetermined path. *Important*: the hunter force is *not* to jump out and attack but merely send the intent to kill. If the tested student senses this correctly and refuses to walk in a particular direction or is clearly wary of a certain area, then this is a direct hit. If the student fails to sense anything, then you will mark this as a negative score.

This exercise should help students recognize their intuitive awareness of threats. Even though this staged threat is not real, it will certainly have a very real negative energy surrounding it. The student who is successful in sensing the contrived danger will certainly be able to sense real danger.

Cleansing through Training

There is a school of thought that suggests that training in *budo* is a rite of purification—the cleansing of the mind and body in preparation for a higher purpose. This is suggested by some of the rites that are practiced when entering and leaving the dojo, and the disciplined behavior that is required within the dojo.

If you are about to enter a Japanese temple the normal procedure would be to cleanse yourself and your energy with the incense smoke that is billowing from a receptacle at the entrance. The thought is that the smoke will cleanse you and purify you of negativity before you enter a sacred place. This is also similar to the cleansing ritual used by shamans or the native Americans. We all have our methods of cleansing. Before I do a reading, I will pray and sometimes have a shower while meditating in order to cleanse myself. On entering the dojo at the *hombu* we will normally take off our shoes. To my mind this is also a method of cleansing away the impurity of the outside world. I know a lot of you will say that removing your shoes is only done to protect the *tatami* (fragile flooring mats found in the dojo), but just ponder this for a while and analyze what we do in the dojo before you agree or disagree. On entering the dojo, we bow and show reverence. Normally, at the front of the dojo, there will be a *kamiza* or *kamidana*, which is the seat of the gods or the wooden temple that is the reflection of divinity. There will be a candle or sometimes incense being burned in order to cleanse and purify the sacred space.

In the same way, we do this when we meditate and even when we train. By training our minds and opening our sixth senses, we naturally raise our vibrations to cleanse and purify mind, body and soul. When we sweat in the dojo and move our energies through the physical exertion that some of the techniques and *kata* require, we throw all of our senses in the middle to dance and be cleansed through that act of joining all facets of our being. Perhaps this is why we feel so good after training: clean on the inside and ready to face the world once more.

The Importance of Listening to Your Inner Wisdom

Connor was a person who was very spiritual and dedicated to the martial way and *bushido*. He'd tried to live the life of a warrior ever since he was old enough to make the choice. He found that the more he dedicated himself to learning the wisdom of the *budo* masters, the more he was spiritually awakening to his own inner wisdom and psychic abilities.

There is an ability that we mediums surrender to regularly, and that is dream state precognition—the ability to foretell events or to receive warnings while sleeping. This is the way that many people receive information, and yet only a handful act upon it.

Connor was one such person who had experienced this phenomenon time and time again, but he'd never listened or recognized that he was receiving information from a higher wisdom. In one case, Connor was considering an attempt to move beyond being "just good friends" with a female associate. Some time before this he started to experience two recurring dreams: in one a train derailed and went over a cliff, and in the other he was in the dojo being defeated in match after match. These dreams could have had several interpretations at the time, but another dream followed a few nights later. This time, he saw an eagle trying to follow an air current upwards but being held back by something undefined holding onto its leg. Unfortunately, Connor didn't make the connection between the dreams and his budding relationship because the dreams had occurred five years prior to his pursuit of the relationship. The romance started well but deteriorated rapidly and became very difficult to get out of without causing significant harm.

We all experience dreams similar to this, but most of us fail to remember them after we wake unless they are very vivid—its those dreams that we should remember. I often tell my students to keep a dream journal at the side of the bed. If you are developing correctly within the dojo and your understanding of *budo* is progressing, then you will naturally be opening yourself up to higher wisdom, and in time you will be able to recognize that wisdom. At certain points in your life—especially after a particularly enlightening session in the dojo—you will begin to dream and receive information from higher wisdom or your own super-consciousness. These dreams should be recorded, for they may hold secrets and answers to your most burning questions.

Becoming Victorious

What does victory mean to you, or to anyone for that matter? In *budo* or in martial arts it is well understood that you become "victorious" if you manage to outwit your opponent and land that punch, kick or strike with a weapon, as this action will score points. The more points you have, the greater your chance to be named the victor at the end of the match. In life we look at victory as conquering something or perhaps winning an item that you covet. The problem is that this is false victory—it's entirely based on material values.

Victory in the dojo is more profound: you can become victorious through overcoming your fears within the dojo or, more importantly, achieving something that you were physically not able to do before. Consider a student who is weak at *ukemi* (rolls and breakfalls). They have this internal fear that stops them from doing the *ukemi* properly—they have an irrational fear of being injured and this is a reflection of life. If they persevere in their training, one day they'll execute the perfect roll—is this not being victorious? We demonstrate shallow-mindedness if we think that victory is only a by-product of conflict.

In *budo* or in any other martial way, victory is realized when we achieve mastery of the self. This is our true goal, and it mirrors what is sought in religion or any spiritual practice that we follow. We aim to achieve mastery of the self—the synergy of all our senses, including our sixth sense, which results in the unification of mind, body and soul.

Therefore, you could make a comparison between the dojo and life. In our lives, we always strive to conquer our fears, overcome our negative emotions, and confront that which would destroy us—the same as in the dojo. You could further recognize that all of life *is* a dojo, and if you become victorious over something small in your training, this will be reflected in the success you will achieve in your life. One of my students managed to overcome much in his own life, making him now the victor and not the defeated.

> *I began my journey in ninjutsu some twenty years ago, back in my native Liverpool. I began attending lessons with a* shodan *friend of mine. When showing me how to tie the belt, he allowed me to borrow his own for practice. He remarked that this was the first and last time I would ever wear a black belt. Being a young man at the time, my ego was still a bit of a problem, so this ruffled my feathers somewhat.*
>
> *I threw myself into my training, but my friend's words seemed to be prophetic when, about nine*

months later, I suffered a minor stroke—putting me firmly out of action. As I recovered from this setback, I did not return to ninjutsu for some reason, but tried my hand at various other styles, though never for very long.

During this time I was fortunate enough to meet and marry a wonderful woman. We moved up to the highlands of Scotland and started a family. As often happens in situations like these, my motivation and free time for training evaporated. Unfortunately, I was further indisposed by a long-standing kidney problem that worsened to the point that I had to undergo procedures to begin peritoneal dialysis. A catheter was inserted into my abdominal cavity, but while this was ongoing, peritonitis set in. This condition went undiagnosed for a long time, and took me to death's door. After emergency surgery, I ended up on a dialysis machine, with the disease having painfully savaged the nerves in my arms and hands, leaving me with little movement or feeling.

The nerves started slowly growing back, but the doctors were never sure how much movement would return. During the long months when I was separated from my family, with my poor wife undergoing terrible hardship raising our children alone and worrying about me, I reached rock bottom and resolved to fight. I decided that once my arms had sufficiently recovered, I would once again train in the martial arts.

Some months after this, my older brother, Steven, was courageous and loving enough to donate a kidney to me, improving my health dramatically.

Long before my arms were anywhere near being recovered, my lovely wife spotted an ad for a samu-

rai- and ninja-based art here in the Highlands. Not only that, but the teacher was more than happy to take on disabled students! Coincidence or fate, I could not ignore this chance. I contacted Jock and arranged to attend my first lesson. During the next few weeks I was pushed and encouraged and discovered that, even with my limited physical ability, I could actually do this! With my family supporting me, and my new friends helping and training me, I improved by leaps and bounds, growing stronger in body and mind.

Years later, having been rigorously taught—physically and spiritually—by Jock, I find myself a much different person than the young man who started the journey in Liverpool (less hair for a start!). I am stronger and more confident in myself than ever before, able to help and encourage students to show what they can overcome in the dojo and life. I can also enjoy my fantastic family and life to the full—despite my disability.

Earlier this year a fellow student, John, and I joined Jock on a journey to Harstadt in Norway. The purpose of the trip was to attend an intense week of physical and spiritual training, which everyone deeply and thoroughly enjoyed. The feedback from the seminar was excellent. At the end of this seminar, I was the owner of a coveted black belt. It's been quite a journey with some interesting times along the way. With grateful thanks to my family and teacher (friend) Jock, one part of my journey has ended, and I confidently look forward to the rest of the ride!

— Andy Saunders

The relationships you forge with others are natural by-products of this victory and mastery of the self, and the respect that is forged within the dojo reflects on those you encounter outside the dojo. Respect is reflected between a master and a student, and within you as well. If you can't respect yourself, then you will not respect others—no matter how much you think you do. A sign of respect in the dojo does not just start with the bow at the beginning of the class or when you meet your partner with whom you are about to practice. Respect starts the minute you consider preparing yourself for training. Suppose you have been training for a while and a new student joins the dojo. Most people—and I have done this myself—think they are above going back to the basics, and so do not extend the hand of friendship as they should right from the start. This withholding behavior denies the new student even a modicum of respect. If we were to consider that we, too, have walked that path, we would show love for the student the way we should—becoming the epitome of respect. We would be able to give of ourselves freely so that others could learn—and of course, we would learn much more in the process. We all have something to teach. A teacher is a student of a master who shares his knowledge and nothing more—it is wrong to put ourselves on a pedestal; by remaining humble we offer respect to our own masters.

Transcending Martial Conflicts

Unfortunately, there is much rivalry in the martial arts, to the point where it mirrors the strife between some of the great world religions. Religion is a man-made thing, it is not a divine gift as some people assert. As in the martial arts, the person following his chosen religion thinks that his is the *only* way and that all others who refuse to follow *the way* are damned for all eternity. This attitude then gives rise to anger, resentment, violence, and—as the worst case scenario—war. Who is to say that one who chooses a path of different belief is damned? We don't have that right. Are we not all part of the same divine spark and creative force of the universe? Is it not true that all paths lead back to the same source? How then can one be wrong in choosing a different path from someone else? Did Jesus or Buddha—who were both real men—come to teach religion and separation? No, they came to teach love for humanity, forgiveness, and unity with the creative force within the universe resulting in mastery of the self. Now, I hope I'm not being silly here, but does that not resemble the path to *budo*?

In essence therefore, no path is "right" or "wrong," for there is no real separation or division between the religions, although most have been saddled with dogmatic beliefs that control through fear and retribution.

Unfortunately, we've called our own jihad (holy war) of sorts within the martial arts to prove who is better or whose style is the most effective. However, as with religion, the main goal of *budo* and the martial way should be self-mastery. To this end we should rise above the self-destructive, man-made materialism and weakness by opening our spiritual gifts. We should stand indivisible, realizing that we all have a part to play and something to teach in order to make this world a harmonious place in which to live.

Conclusion

Budo and martial arts have no separation from the intuitive aspects of the self or indeed our own individual lives. Our intuition or psychic abilities are the final key with which we are able to unlock the door of self-mastery—the ultimate goal of the warrior. It is important to realize that the "missing link" is not really missing—for all answers are within. As with physical training in the dojo; it takes dedication and effort to unlock the door and begin on the path to change and self-discovery.

In developing our intuitive faculties we not only increase our chances of remaining safe in a hostile world, but we also raise our vibrations to such an extent that we unlock the hidden secrets of *budo.* We discover the methods needed to bring together mind, body, and soul—forged to work as one whole being. We rise above mediocrity and materialist beliefs that hold us prisoner. We see the beauty in the unseen world and observe the divinity in nature. Our own spirituality becomes harmoniously forged through physical and mental discipline in the dojo. We follow no dogma but rather listen to the beating heart of *budo*. Victory is not found in the destruction of an enemy—that's "winning." Victory is found in your personal growth and mastery within the *kukan* (void), resulting in the unity of mind and body.

An important lesson to understand is that the sixth sense is not a gift reserved for psychics, mediums, magicians, healers or the spiritually elite. The sixth sense does not exist for a select few to divine hidden information using occult tools, instead; it is a gift given by God to every man, woman, and child. It is innate in everyone, and is the key to the hidden gems of the universe. You have the free will to decide whether to develop this gift or not, but given that the choice could be the difference between life and death—is there really a choice?

Budo is much more than learning how to fight; it is learning how to apply lessons from the dojo to the totality of our lives. If we open our inner eyes, our experiences in the dojo can teach us all about life and how to deal with its daily challenges. Life *is* a dojo, and the virtues to be had within could indeed show the way to a safer, more peaceful world.

Bibliography

Bolelli, D. *On the Warriors Path.* Berkeley, California: Blue Snake Books, 2008.

Brocas, J. *Power of the Sixth Sense: How to Keep Safe in a Hostile World.* Great Britain: O Books, 2008.

Hanh, T. N. *Anger.* New York: Riverhead Trade, 2002.

_______. *Peace is Every Step: The Path of Mindfulness in Everyday Life.* New York: Bantam Books, 1991.

_______. *The Miracle of Mindfulness.* Boston, Massachusetts: Bea con Press, 1975.

Hatsumi, M. *Essence of Ninjutsu: The Nine Traditions.* Columbus, Ohio: McGraw-Hill, 1988.

_______. *Ninjutsu: History and Traditions.* California: Unique Publications, 1982.

_______. *Ten Ryaku No Maaki.*

Kaufman, S. *Musashi's Book of Five Rings.* Rutland, Vermont: Tuttle Publishing, 2004.

McTaggart, L. *The Field: The Quest for the Secret Force of the Universe.* Great Britain: HarperCollins Publishers, 2003.

Sheldrake, R. *The Sense of Being Stared At.* New York: Three Rivers Press, 2004.

Targ, R. www.espresearch.com

About the Author

Jock Brocas is an internationally renowned psychic medium who uniquely blends spirituality with the teachings of *budo*. Jock has been a *budo* practitioner for many years and has been guided by many fine teachers, both spiritually and physically. He believes in the power of *budo* to offer the keys to changing one's life for the better. He finds the combat aspects of the martial path to be just one small facet of training, and believes that the mind is the best weapon. To be most effective, the mind, body, and spirit must join as one spiritual unit. Jock regularly teaches and lectures in workshops around the world, focusing on the powerful way that life lessons from *budo* can serve to enhance the life of the spirit. Our spirituality allows us to overcome obstacles and proves that no matter your creed, color or health; everyone has an innate power that can be part of what makes the world a beautiful place to live. Learn more at www.bookofsixrings.com.